DEESIDE

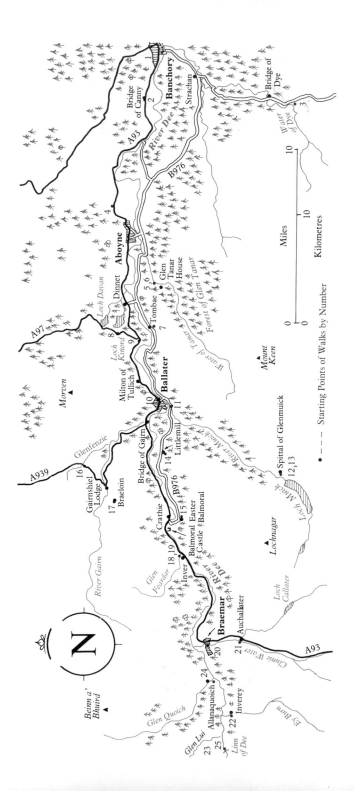

25 WALKS

DEESIDE

Robert Smith

Series Editor: Roger Smith

Aberdeen Tourist Board

EDINBURGH:HMSO

First published 1994

Applications for reproduction should be made to HMSO

Acknowledgements

A word of thanks to the people who have helped in the compilation of this book, particularly Alistair and Evis Ritchie; Mrs Judith Lewis, Secretary of the Scottish Rights of Way Society; and my wife, Sheila.

Thanks are due to Grampians Highlands and Aberdeen for their help in the preparation of the text and for the supply of cover and additional transparencies

British Library Cataloguing in Publication Data

A catalogue record for this book is available from the British Library

Cover illustration: Invercauld Bridge (Grampian Highlands and Aberdeen)

ISBN 0 11 495158 6

CONTENTS

USEFUL INFORMATION

The length of each walk is given in kilometres and miles, but within the text measurements are metric for simplicity. The walks are described in detail and are supported by accompanying maps (study them before you start the walk), so there is little likelihood of getting lost, but if you want a back-up you will find the 1:25 000 Pathfinder Ordnance Survey maps on sale locally.

Every care has been taken to make the descriptions and maps as accurate as possible, but the author and publishers can accept no responsibility for errors, however caused. The countryside is always changing and there will inevitably be alterations to some aspects of these walks as time goes by. The publishers and author would be happy to receive comments and suggested alterations for future editions of the book.

METRIC MEASUREMENTS

At the beginning of each walk, the distance is given in miles and kilometres. Within the text, all measurements are metric for simplicity (and indeed our Ordnance Survey maps are now all metric). However, it was felt that a conversion table might be useful to those readers who, like the author, still tend to think in Imperial terms.

The basic statistic to remember is that one kilometre is five-eighths of a mile. Half a mile is equivalent to 800 metres and a quarter-mile is 400 metres. Below that distance, yards and metres are little different in practical terms.

km	miles
1	0.625
1.6	1
2	1.25
3	1.875
3.2	2
4	2.5
4.8	3
5	3.125
6	3.75
6.4	4
7	4.375
8	5
9	5.625
10	6.25
16	10

INTRODUCTION

Royal Deeside is a walker's paradise – the 'dear Paradise' that Queen Victoria discovered when she came north last century to make Balmoral her Scottish home. It is a land of magnificent mountains and romantic glens, and it is also castle country, with a rich and colourful history. This book takes you on 25 Deeside walks, from Banchory near Aberdeen to Braemar and the edge of the Cairngorms.

It gives you a taste of the wild places, but you don't have to be a hardened hillwalker or Munro-bagger to enjoy it. The walks are well within the capability of anyone who is reasonably fit, and most are suitable for children. They range in length from 6 to 16 kilometres (4 to 10 miles).

The weather in this part of Scotland, particularly as you get near to the hills, can be changeable, so you should go dressed for whatever Nature offers. Waterproofs are advised for all the walks – just in case. For some of them strong walking shoes or hill boots are necessary. Information at the beginning of each walk gives advice on clothing and footwear.

Part of the pleasure of walking is in knowing about the countryside around you . . . its history, its flora and fauna, its myths and legends. This book takes you on the trail of the Haunted Stag, along a wooded track of the Warlock's stone, and up by 'lonely, lonely dark Loch Kander'. You will cross the Seven Brigs, search for the Seven Wells, and picnic by shiels once used by Queen Victoria.

If you have a dog make sure it is under control – keep it on the lead in areas where there may be deer, grouse or other wildlife.

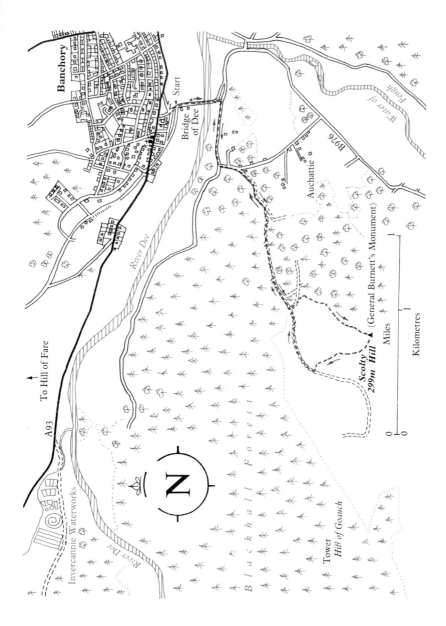

SCOLTY HILL

S colty Hill, on the outskirts of Banchory, might have remained a small and undistinguished peak if someone hadn't put a tower on top of it. That was in 1842, when the tower was erected in memory of General William Burnett of Banchory Lodge. Since then, Scolty's tower has been a familiar landmark on Lower Deeside.

It has also been a favourite walk for both locals and visitors. To get there, walk down Banchory's Dee Street and cross the Bridge of Dee, bearing left on the A943, then turn sharp right up the Auchattie road. You can cut the corner by climbing a stepped path opposite the south end of the bridge. About 500m up the Auchattie road, turn left at the junction signposted Scolty Hill and look for a rough road branching off about 150m ahead.

Follow this road until you see another track bearing right (there is usually a pole barrier across it) and if you

INFORMATION

Distance return: 6 km (4 miles), with 220m ascent.

Start and finish: Bridge Street, Banchory. See text for details of approach to Scolty.

Terrain: Mostly good track, rougher on final climb to the summit. Boots or strong shoes recommended.

Refreshments: Wide choice in Banchory.

Toilets: In Banchory.

Information: Tourist information centre in the car park at Bridge Street.

Scolty tower.

are driving you can leave your car there. Take the right-hand track, ignoring other paths, until you see a 'Scolty' sign pointing uphill to where a wooden gate bars the way. Through that lies the final push to the top of Scolty.

Looking across to Banchory from Scolty.

Once through the gate, go left for 150m, keeping your eye open for a footpath on the right. This leads up the hill through open woodlands of birch, interspersed with Scots pine, with the fenced-in Forestry Commission plantation on the left. The track gets steeper and stonier the higher you climb. Finally, the tower is seen over the brow of the hill, the trees are left behind, and you are up on the bare Scolty plateau.

The tower is built on a large circular area of ground, with two indicators picking out the distant hills – Peter Hill in the Forest of Birse; the familiar lump of Clachnaben; Clachan Yell, rising above Glen Tanar; Mount Keen, the most easterly of the Munros; and a handful of lesser peaks. The indicator on the other side points to Morven, Mortlich and even the humble Tyrebagger at Aberdeen.

Banchory lies below, stretching out from the winding Dee. This Deeside town, which has become almost a dormitory for Aberdeen, must have been a good deal smaller and less lively when the tower was erected in 1842 by General Burnett's 'numerous friends and tenantry'. He died three years earlier, in 1839, at the age of 72. He was a veteran of the Napoleonic Wars. Not much has been written about him, but he was said to be 'a public spirited gentleman and a kind landlord, whose memory will be long and gratefully cherished in this neighbourhood'.

Until recently, one thing was missing from the Scolty tower – it had no staircase. Then a helicopter came clattering over the hill and neatly lowered one into the tower. Now, visitors can climb up the metal steps and get an even loftier bird's eye view of the surrounding countryside. The Prince of Wales came along to have a look at it. There is a plaque on the tower commemorating his visit on 15th September 1992, 'on the occasion of the 150th anniversary and the restoration of the monument by the Rotary Club of Banchory Ternan'.

Plaque commemorating Prince Charles's visit to Scolty.

Scolty Tower looks down on the vast expanse of Blackhall Forest. Blackhall, which today covers some 1200 hectares, once boasted a castle – Blackhall Castle, originally the seat of the Bannerman family. It was in fact, a pseudo-castle, a mansion house built in the castellated style, and was eventually demolished. From Scolty you can see the Invercannie waterworks, which supplies Aberdeen with its water. In the days when timber was brought down the Dee in log-rafts, one of the most difficult parts of the journey was the 'Glisters', on the Blackhall Castle stretch opposite the waterworks.

The woods around Scolty were planted in 1941 to replace large-scale felling by Canadian lumberjacks during the last war. Although Blackhall is Forestry Commission property, the top of Scolty is owned by a local farmer. This comes about because the bare ground around the summit forms part of the farmlands of Ardlair, which lies south of the hill.

Paths can be seen running across the neighbouring slopes towards the oddly-named Hill of Goauch and on to the Shooting Greens on the west side of the forest, but these should be left to hill-walkers and runners who know the area. There are other paths in Blackhall that can be explored, but the only one of consequence to Scolty walkers, apart from the climb up the hill, is one which drops down the west side and circles round it to join the main path at the wooden gate. From there it is a straight walk back to the car.

The return route opens up a striking view of the country to the north of the River Dee, and particularly the long ridge of the Hill of Fare.

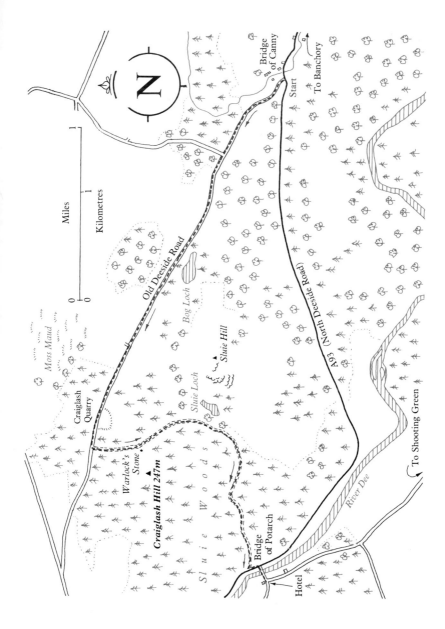

Bridge of Canny

To Banchory

Start

Old Deeside Road

A93 (North Deeside Road)

Bog Loch

Sluie Hill

Sluie Hill

Sluie Loch

Moss Maud

Craiglash Quarry

Warlock's Stone

Craiglash Hill 247m

S l u i e   W o o d s

River Dee

To Shooting Green

Bridge of Potarch

Hotel

Miles

Kilometres

N

CRAIGLASH

When witch-hunting mania swept the north-east in the late 16th century, Deeside was one of the areas noted for 'the detestabil practize of witchcraft'. It spread right up the valley. Craig Coillich at Ballater was at one time known as the Witch's Hill, and five miles to the east, witches were burned at the stake on Creag nam Ban. But Craiglash Hill, near Torphins, was the most notorious haunt of witches and warlocks. Even now, it is no place to be on a dark night. It is the sort of setting in which you would expect to meet 'ghosties and ghoulies and things that go bump in the night'. But in daylight hours it is a different scene.

Despite Craiglash's murky history, one of the most pleasant short walks on Lower Deeside can be found on the hill. It runs to Potarch, which was an important halting place for drovers heading south for the cattle trysts . . . and it passes the spot where witches held their covens 300 years ago.

From the Bridge of Canny, about 3km west of Banchory, a minor road goes off to join the Torphins-Kincardine O'Neil road. This is the Old Deeside Road, the original highway up the Dee valley, which was virtually wiped from the map with the coming of turnpikes. Now it is little more than a short cut for motorists going from Banchory to Torphins. G. M. Fraser, author of *The Old Deeside Road*, described it is 'a

INFORMATION

Distance return: 8 km (5 miles).

Start and finish: On the Craiglash road near the Bog Loch. An alternative start point is the Bridge of Canny, west of Banchory on the A93.

Terrain: Good road and track. No special footwear needed.

Refreshments: Potarch Hotel is at the end of the walk. Wide selection in Banchory.

Potarch Bridge.

splendid walking road along its whole length'. That was in 1921, and today, if you don't mind the traffic, it is still true, but it isn't necessary to walk the whole length of the road.

Take your car up part of the way, and 1.5km from the Bridge of Canny you will see on the left a wooden gate where a track goes down through the trees to a dark pool called the Bog Loch – evil things are said to have happened there. From here you continue along the old road on foot. There is plenty of space to park in an unofficial lay-by on the right-hand side of the road opposite the gate. Heavily wooded, the area you are going through looks like the ideal setting for a gathering of witches and warlocks. The woods open out into a stretch of countryside dominated by peat mosses. Away to the right is desolate Moss Maud, where they say a 'Heidless Horseman' drove terrified travellers off the old road into the water-filled peat-hags.

A mile from the wooden gate is Craiglash Quarry, where a monstrous hole has been gouged out of the hill. The road goes through the quarry, and a short distance past it a track turns off to the left. This is the way to Potarch. The track climbs gently away from the quarry road, then dips and rises again, and among the trees on the right-hand side can be seen a gigantic stone. This is 'the gryt stane of Craigleuch' – the Warlock's Stone.

Warlock's Stone.

The stone was the meeting place of a Deeside coven of witches. Their names appear in the records of witchcraft trials held in Aberdeen in 1596–97, when 23 women and one man – the warlock, Colin Massie – were convicted of witchcraft and condemned to death. Some were publicly strangled by the hangman, others were burned at the stake. 'Vitch roastin' was a popular spectator sport in those days.

The 'gyrt stane' lies in two parts. How it came to be split is a mystery. One theory put forward was that it was broken in two to discourage any return to witchcraft in the area, but it would have taken a superhuman effort to do that. The smaller section has been chopped off like the top of an egg.

The track to Potarch winds its way down towards the Dee between Craiglash and Sluie Hill. The Bog-loch of Sluie was named as one of the places where the witches met. The woods bordering the drovers' route are known as the Sluie Woods, but they have little resemblance to the dense forest that existed in the 16th century.

When the sun breaks through the trees, all thoughts of 'ane devilische danss with Sathan' are pushed aside. There are no warlocks lurking in the woods nowadays as you go down to the Dee. The river comes into view. Turn left when you reach the North Deeside road (A93) and you will see Potarch Bridge, where at one time there were spooks, not witches. A mischievous water-kelpie haunted the ancient ferry over the Dee, but disappeared when the bridge was built.

At Potarch, the great North Road over the Cairn o' Mount formerly crossed the river at Inchbare, a little below the bridge. It was at this ford that Edward I crossed the Dee on his way to and from Kildrummy. The drovers going south went over the Shooting Greens from Potarch (there are Forestry Commission walks there now) and headed for Whitestone on Feughside before driving their cattle over the 'Cairn'. The green at Potarch was the scene of one of the many old-time fairs held on Deeside, and in more recent years it became a mecca for weekend trippers from Aberdeen. Eventually, with campers and caravanners making the place look like a fairground, the authorities banned overnight stays, but it is still a very popular picnic area.

At Potarch Inn, which serves thirsty trippers instead of drovers, there is no Warlock's Stone to attract visitors, but there are 'gryt stones' of another kind outside the door. These are the Dinnie stones, the practice weights used by the world-famous Deeside heavyweight athlete, Donald Dinnie, when he trained at Potarch. Dinnie was able to carry the stones across Potarch Bridge with little trouble. Many people have tried to do the same. No one has succeeded, although a handful of people have been able to lift them.

Dinnie stones at Potarch Hotel.

The return to your car from Potarch is by the same route.

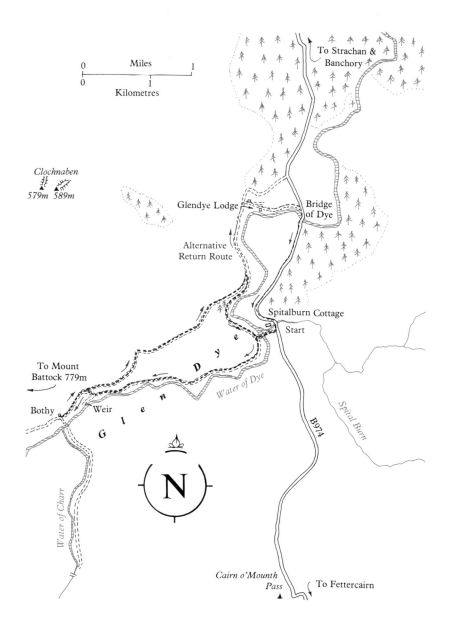

Miles

Kilometres

Clochnaben
579m   589m

To Strachan &
Banchory

Glendye Lodge

Bridge
of Dye

Alternative
Return Route

Spitalburn Cottage

Start

Water of Dye

To Mount
Battock 779m

Bothy

Weir

G l e n   D y e

Water of Charr

B974

Spital Burn

N

*Cairn o' Mounth
Pass*

To Fettercairn

GLEN DYE

The giant tor on the 579m Clachnaben, south of the Deeside village of Strachan (pronounced Stra-an), can be seen from most parts of Lower Deeside. Its wart-like rock, 29m high, looks down on the Cairn o' Mounth pass, which for centuries has been a main artery from Deeside to the south. Ten kilometres from Strachan the road crosses a bridge spanning the Spital Burn, a tributary of the Water of Dye. Here, as the name Spital indicates, there was once a hospice serving travellers going over the Cairn o' Mounth. Now there is only a ruined cottage, but this tranquil spot is the starting point of a walk through a glen whose scenery is in sharp contrast to the naked moors around Clachnaben. There is an old ballad which says:

> *The Cairn-na-Mounth is bleak and bare*
> *An' cauld is Cloch-na-bane.*

The Spital wasn't always tranquil. The hospice later became a public house, a haunt of thieves, and robberies were common on the highway, but in time the intimation was made in Strachan church: 'The Cairn o' Mount road is quite safe now. There's honest folk at the Spital'.

Just past the Spital bridge, on the right-hand side of the road, a track goes down about 200m to a fence and locked gate. The fence is surmounted by a high, awkward stile. Take care going over it. Once on the other side, a wooden bridge crosses the Water of Dye and a short distance further on, the track meets up with another coming in on the right from Glendye Lodge. Turn left here.

The route follows the river, with woods and pleasant haughland below. This is what Joseph Grant, a well-known Deeside writer, had in mind in 1869 when he wrote about 'the beautiful valley of Glen Dye – an oasis in a desert'. But the 'matchless' scenery gradually gives way to moorland. On the right, where a gap in the hills opens up a view of Clachnaben, a solitary tree can be seen in the middle of an area where there are crumbling stone dykes and the ruins of a cottage.

INFORMATION

Distance return:
8 km (5 miles). Add 4 km (2.5 miles) for return via Glendye Lodge.

Start and finish:
Spital Burn (GR 647847). Take the B974 from Banchory to Strachan and turn left over the bridge as you enter Strachan (signed to Fettercairn). Spital Burn is 10 km (6 miles) from Strachan.

Terrain: Good track all the way. No special footwear needed.

Refreshments: None en route. There is a cafe at Clatterin' Brig, at the southern foot of the Cairn o'Mount road.

The Fasque bothy in Glen Dye.

Curiously, Joseph Robertson described how, in a field near the 'highway', a lone tree marked the spot where the cottage and kailyard of a notorious warlock, Colin Massie, once stood (see Craiglash, walk 2). Massie's mother and brother lived with him in Glen Dye. Was this the same place? No one knows, but there is certainly an odd sense of desolation about it.

Keep an eye open on the high tops to the left, where red deer are often seen grazing. As you head along the track you will see a group of buildings in the distance. One of them is the Charr bothy, at the junction of the Water of Charr and the Dye. Nearer to it, not far from a weir on the Dye, the track turns sharp right, goes uphill for a short distance, and then turns left to the bothy.

Fasque bothy in Glen Dye.

The bothy is bare but solidly wind and waterproof, which is all that the majority of hill-walkers want. From the entries in the visitors' book it would seem that most people are happy enough with it – 'Great bothy for the kids', read one entry. As a plaque on the door indicates, Fasque Estates handed over the care of the building to the Mountain Bothies Association, the funding being provided by the 'family and friends of the late John Whitley'.

This link with the MBA is interesting, for another entry dated 9 January 1993 notes that it was 'Jim Cosgrove's Birthday Party'. Jim Cosgrove, who hails from Letham in Angus, is well known to hill-walkers; he is a veteran member of both the MBA and the Scottish Rights of Way Society. He has done a one-man repair job on many bothies in the north-east. It was his 80th birthday that the Charr party was celebrating.

There is a kind of wind-break wall outside the front door and you can sit there in the sun, feet up, and look across to where the Water of Charr comes tumbling down from the hills. The track beside the river, going south, leads eventually to the Clatterin' Brig at the foot of the Cairn o' Mount.

Behind the bothy the track from the Spital pushes on towards Mount Battock, into wild and desolate hill-country. This is for hardier and more experienced hillwalkers. Your route is in the opposite direction, back the way you came; for a start, at any rate. Where the track turns down to the river, take another track going straight ahead, running parallel with the track from the Spital. Like the old song, you will be taking the 'high road' back to your starting point, while on the way out you took the 'low road'.

The 'high road' gives a new perspective on Clachnaben (or Clochnaben) country. Away in the distance you can see traffic crawling up the Cairn o' Mount, heading for Fettercairn. The land around it is bleak and bare, as the old ballad says, and the contrasting gentleness of Glen Dye underlines this. Yet in some ways it has a kind of wild beauty of its own, with the old Clach sticking its knotted head up defiantly among the surrounding hills.

Clachnaben from Glen Dye.

The road back climbs steadily, then drops down and heads for Glendye Lodge, which is 5 km from the Charr bothy. After passing a small belt of trees, about 1.5 km from the lodge, it links up with another track coming up from the Water of Dye. This is the track that takes you back to Spital Burn. This route down the hill runs close to the Dye, which at times can be an angry river. When a move was made to introduce a toll on the Bridge of Dye in 1685, a petition said that there were times when the Water of Dye 'damnifies the bridge exceedingly'.

The last lap brings you back to where you first set out on the Glen Dye track after crossing the wooden bridge over the Dye. Now you cross it a second time. Your last obstacle is the high stile below the Cairn o' Mounth road. You have come full circle – and there's honest folk at the Spital!

As an alternative to returning to the Spital you can continue on the 'high road' to Glendye Lodge. On the last stretch you will get a magnificent view of Clachnaben. It means, however, that you will have to walk a mile on the main Cairn o' Mount road to get back to your car.

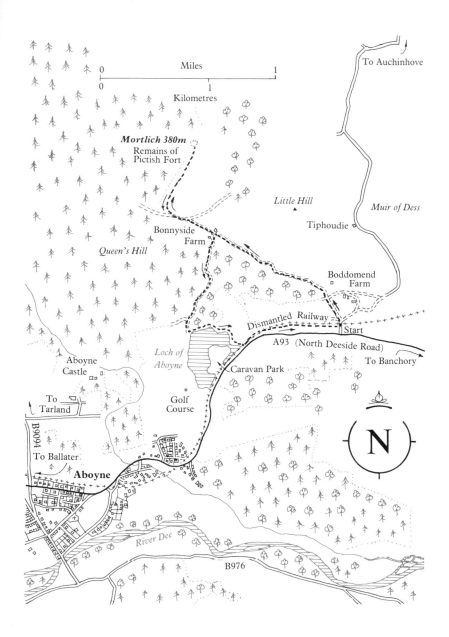

HILL OF MORTLICH

They say there is a ghost on the Hill of Mortlich at Aboyne. Back in 1900, the writer A. I. McConnochie carried a poem about him in his book, *Deeside*. He was a fearsome spectre, it said, 'clad wi' hair', with a beard that was 'three feet an mair', and he was called the Red Cap o' Mortlich.

There have been no sightings of the Red Cap for many years, but if you decide to go and look for him you are not likely to regret it. For, ghost or no ghost, a visit to this 380m hill takes you on one of the most interesting and enjoyable walks in the Aboyne area. About a mile from the Loch of Aboyne, on the A93 road from Aboyne to Banchory, a sign points to Auchinhove and Kirkton Cottages.

Coming from Aboyne, turn left at the sign and cross the old Deeside line. Park near here – there is plenty of space just off the road, which turns right to Boddomend Farm. The route to Mortlich, however, is straight ahead, up a rough farm track that curves away to the left, passing a stretch of woodland. There is a gate across the track just before you reach a small quarry.

Beyond the quarry the road climbs steadily, opening up a magnificent view of Aboyne and its loch, with the Deeside hills in the background. A young forestry plantation can be seen in the fields on the right. Farther on, a redstone track breaks off on the left and goes downhill to the farm of Bonnyside, which comes into view as you continue on the higher track. The farm makes a mockery of its name. Set snugly in a hollow on the moor, it must have been a wealthy farmtown at one time, but now it is desolate and abandoned, looking as if its only use would be as a haunt of the ghostly Red Cap. The buildings are in ruins, with tumbling roofs and broken windows. Bonnyside, left to the wind and weather, is bonny no more.

INFORMATION

Distance: 7 km (4 ½ miles), with 260m ascent.

Start and finish: Old Deeside railway line near Boddomend Farm, which is 1.5km from Loch of Aboyne on the A93. See text for details.

Terrain: Track and path. Boots or strong shoes advised. Take waterproofs.

Refreshments: None en route. Good selection in Aboyne.

Tourist Centre There is pike fishing on the Loch of Aboyne. Contact the Warden at Aboyne Loch Caravan Park. The tourist information centre in the Ballater Road car park is open daily from Easter to mid-September.

Ruined Bonnyside Farm.

Go past the farm and follow a less distinct path which takes you through a gate and on towards woodland on the Queen's Hill. Before you reach the wood the path splits, the left-hand leg going through the wood and coming out on a back road linking Coull with the Tarland road. It is a walk worth doing another time. Meantime, however, your way is along the right-hand path and up the hill through the woods, sticking closely to a fence on the left.

Walkers sit by the ruined monument on Mortlich Hill.

The path, although indeterminate in parts, goes all the way to the top, the final push being a hard one. Small pine trees thin out as you reach the heather-clad summit. The great pile of stones on top scarcely adds to Mortlich's glory, yet at one time this modest peak – the highest point in the parish – was a conspicuous landmark in the district.

The reason was that it was surmounted by a granite obelisk 20 m high, with a metal cross on top of it. The monument was erected in 1868 to the memory of Charles, 10th Marquis of Huntly, whose ancestral home, Aboyne Castle, is about half a mile north of the village. Now, all that is left of the monument is a heap of rubble. No one would know that it had ever been there unless they stumbled on the clues among the stones. One is a large piece of metal sticking up among the boulders, the remains of the crown that topped the obelisk. The other is a flat rectangular stone with a faded inscription on it. It tells how the monument was raised by the Marquis's widow, Mary Antoinetta, and 'the Tenantry of Aboyne'. He died on 18th September 1863.

What happened to the monument is a bit of a mystery. On 7th November 1912, the *Aberdeen Daily Journal* reported with a faint air of surprise that the obelisk was no longer there. 'Yesterday morning', it said, 'early risers in Aboyne, on looking towards the Hill of Mortlich, were astonished to find that the monument erected on the hill in 1864 in memory of a former Marquis was gone. On investigation being made, it was found that the monument had collapsed. The wet weather and the fact that the edifice was in need of repairs were, it is said, responsible for its collapse'.

So much for lost glory. There is another piece of forgotten history buried under these stones, for a Pictish fort once stood on Mortlich's summit. A. I.

McConnochie mentioned seeing the remains of a large enclosure there, but there is little sign of it now. A Pictish road could also be traced from Little Hill, on Mortlich's south-eastern slope, down to Tilphoudie and the Muir of Dess.

Whatever its history, Mortlich is a good place to take stock of Deeside. You look down over the rooftops of Aboyne, on its loch and golf course, and on the great panoramic sweep of the Dee Valley. From little Mortlich, too, you can turn full circle and nod respectfully to the big hills – Lochnagar, Morven, lumpy Clachnaben (Clochnaben), conical Mount Keen, and a few more. The way back from Mortlich is by Bonnyside, but by a different route. Watch out for birds in the woods. Quails have sometimes been seen here, running awkwardly through the bracken and giving out their peculiar whit, whit, whit call.

Part of the metal crown from the Mortlich monument.

Go down the side of the farm and join the redstone track, which runs into the woods beyond the farm buildings. A short distance on, where the track swings right, leave it and go straight ahead along a narrower grassy path. Further on, it turns through a gateway and into the wood, and in a few minutes you will be out on the hill above the golf course looking down on the Loch of Aboyne.

Swans and ducks can often be seen feeding on the loch, which is used by the Aberdeen Water Ski Club. Back in the good old days a different kind of sport took place here – curling. Great 'bonspiels' were held, drawing competitors from far and wide. Part of the old Deeside railway line was used as a 'halt' for the curlers, and you can still see the platform where they disembarked from the train and stepped straight onto the ice.

Loch of Aboyne.

When you reach the edge of the loch turn left and, crossing a stile near the skiers' clubrooms, make your way up a path which opens on to the North Deeside Road (A93). Your route, however, is a quieter one, along the old railway line. Here, the Deeside line hasn't been developed, as it has been nearer Ballater, but it is in reasonable condition – and maybe all the better for being a little wild. What's more, it takes you out where you began, on the road to Boddomend Farm, with your car waiting to take you home.

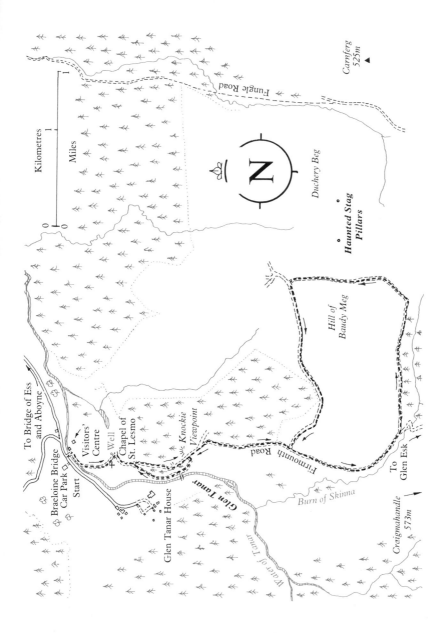

HAUNTED STAG

When a deer-hunting laird called Sir William Cunliffe Brooks took over the Deeside estate of Glen Tanar in 1869 he built fences to keep the deer in, not out. Trophies from the 'shoots' held in those days can still be seen in Glen Tanar House, where the ceiling of the ballroom is studded with over 500 sets of antlers and stags' heads. Under each is a tiny plaque recording the name of the hunter and the date. But one trophy is missing – the head of the Haunted Stag.

This walk takes you on the trail of the Haunted Stag, back in time to a fascinating and little-known episode in the Glen Tanar story. It starts at the Braeloine car park. Cross the old hump-back bridge on the opposite side of the road (once over, the Visitor Centre is on the left) and turn right where a huge copper beech tree guards the approach to the bridge. Waymarked routes are signposted near the bridge. Follow the red marker, which takes you along a track by the Water of Tanar. The grass on either side has been allowed to grow wild, so that in summer the start of the route is garlanded by buttercups, white and pink clover, and other wild flowers.

INFORMATION

Distance: 10 km (6 miles).

Start and finish: Car park at Braeloine Bridge, on the Glen Tanar Estate. Take the B976 South Deeside Road from Aboyne to the Bridge of Ess (about 2.5km) and drive up the estate road to the car park.

Terrain: Part of the walk is over rough tracks, some of it uphill. Boots recommended. Take waterproofs.

Opening hours
Braeloine Interpretive Centre, Glen Tanar: 10.00-17.00 daily, Apr-Sept.

Chapel of St Lesmo.

The track swings round towards the Chapel of St Lesmo, built by William Cunliffe Brooks in 1870. The pews of this beautiful chapel, still used to-day, are lined with deerskin. At one time antlers hung from its ceiling. The old house of Braeloine stood on the site in earlier days, the centre-piece of a busy community known as Braeloine and Knockieside. It dated back to the early 17th century, but now there is nothing to show that it was ever there. A stile takes you over the fence to the Chapel, and at the edge of the track an information board tells the story of Knockieside.

Keeper's stone at St Lesmo.

The graves of the old lairds lie outside the chapel. Beside the dyke around the chapel a long, high stone stands at the grave of Donald MacKintosh, Cunliffe Brooks' gamekeeper. The two men often sat at this stone while out shooting in the hills, and it was agreed that whoever died first would have it at his graveside. In May 1876, Donald was the first to go; the laird kept his promise and had the stone taken down from the hill to his keeper's burial place.

On the opposite side of the track are the remains of an old well once used by travellers going south. Beyond the chapel, the track turns right and heads up Knockie Hill through a plantation of Scots pine and larch –

watch for the red waymarker. Near the gate at the entrance to the woodland is another information board which says that the hill has been used by people at least since the Bronze Age, 4,500 years ago.

The climb up through the woodland is a gentle one, emerging at the Knockie Viewpoint. Here, an indicator board picks out the hills stretching away to the west. A rough track goes downhill towards Glen Tanar House, following the red waymarker, but your route lies straight ahead, with a lofty view of the estate on the right. Glen Tanar House can be seen through the trees, with a small loch near it where visitors can fish for trout.

The track you are following is the Firmounth Road, the old hill road from Deeside to Glenesk. Near a gate on the left you will see a stone carrying the inscription 'Let Well Alone', one of many inscribed stones scattered throughout the estate (see Walk 6), while further on, near a water tank on the right, is another stone marking the site of the Monk's Well. Walking this ancient path you get some idea of the vastness of Glen Tanar Estate, and of the part afforestation has played in it. In the early years of last century it was famous for its fir, large quantities being cut and marketed for timber. The logs were floated down the Water of Tanar, and a ship named the *Countess of Aboyne* was built entirely of timber from the estate.

During the last war 3,200,000 cubic feet of timber was felled in Glen Tanar. Now, as you tramp along the Firmounth, you can see new plantations spreading away to the south. At one time you might also have sniffed whisky in the air, for, like many Deeside glens, illegal whisky-making was rampant in Glen Tanar. The *Aberdeen Free Press* once reported that in the morning you could 'count the "reek" of 13 stills rising from the hillsides on the estate'.

Down in the glen, as you walk, the Tanar can be seen winding its way towards the Dee, while keeping it company is a track which runs into the hills to join the Firmounth. This is a fruitful area for bird-watchers. Redstart and cuckoo are among the summer visitors, and you might also spot crossbills and capercaillies, which depend on Scots pine for food.

Less than a mile from the Knockie Viewpoint, a rough, stony track comes down from the Hill of Baudy Meg. Your return route will take you back to Braeloine by this track, but for the moment ignore it. Instead, head along the Firmounth track until it reaches a fork about 3 km from your starting point at Braeloine. Here, a sign points to the route where the Firmounth path drops down to the Burn of Skinna, crosses it and climbs steeply up through woodlands to the face of Craigmahandle, where it pushes its way over the hill s to Glen Esk.

But your route is by the left-hand fork, where the track passes an old bothy on the right and turns uphill on its way to Baudy Meg. Don't get the wrong idea – there is no one called Meg waiting for you on top. The name comes from the Gaelic *badan magh*, which mea ns the hill of hares. You may see plenty of hares on the Glen Tanar Estate, but no bawdy ladies.

Near here, on Duchery Beg, you will also see the Haunted Stag, or, at least, two stone pillars that mark the spot where it died. The track uphill is rough and stony, and a stiff push. Look away to your right and you will see Carnferg, a hill with a monument on top of it. When you are in line with this monument, you will be able to pick out the pillars in the heather. They are not far beyond a line of shooting butts and a yellow waymarker post which you pass.

William Cunliffe Brooks gave the stag its 'haunted' tag because it was a defiant animal, always escaping his gun, almost as if it was one of the mythical haunted stags that are often said to be seen in the hills. He was never able to get it in his sights long enough to bring it down. Then, on 9th October 1877, he hunted it high on Duchery Beg, where the moor stretches away to Carnferg and the old Fungle pass. Not far off the track is a pillar with a huge stone ball on top of it. This marks the spot where Cunliffe Brooks stood when he fired the fatal shot. Farther away, deep in the heather, is a similar pillar and ball. It stands 267 feet (81m) from the first pillar - the exact distance at which Cunliffe Brooks shot his elusive stag.

In those days a 'kill' at this distance was regarded as a considerable feat, and Cunliffe Brooks, who was never

One of the Haunted Stag stones.

known for his modesty, erected his own monument to commemorate the event; two monuments, to be exact. Faded inscriptions on the stone balls carry the words 'The Haunted Stag', and then declare, 'The Stag is dead. Sure bullet to its fatal mark hath sped'.

Jimmy Oswald, Glen Tanar's present head keeper, has a record of the Haunted Stag's shooting in his Game Book, but the whereabouts of the antlers is a mystery. It is thought that they might have been among the antlers that once hung in St Lesmo Chapel. These were later removed when it was decided that the antlers of dead deer were not the most suitable adornments for a place of worship.

Continue along the track, keeping an eye open for an overgrown track going sharply off to the left. Take this track, which runs along the side of Baudy Meg and drops down to the track you were on earlier - the Firmounth Road. The last part of the old track is stony, sandy and often slippery, so care has to be taken. Once back on the Firmounth track, retrace your steps to the Knockie Viewpoint and go downhill to the Tanar Water, near Glen Tanar House. Turn right, cross a cattle grid and go through a gate straight ahead of you. This takes you to the start of the Knockie plantation, where the path turns off past St Lesmo Chapel and back to Braeloine and the car park.

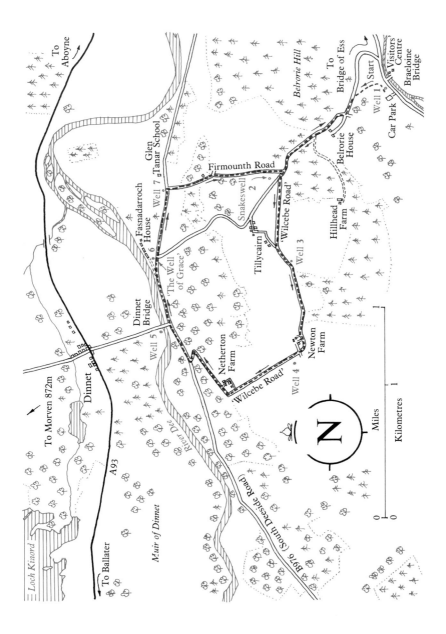

WILCEBE ROAD

The name 'Wilcebe Road' has never appeared in any map or guidebook. The road is on Belrorie Hill, in Glen Tanar Estate, and was coined from the initials of an eccentric 19th century laird, William Cunliffe Brooks. Will C. Brooks . . . Will C.B. . . . Wilcebe. The initials WCB can be seen on wells, seats, walls and stones all over the estate, along with cryptic homilies to passers-by. One near the entrance to the glen warns 'Beware of the Deer' while another reads 'Honest water never left man in the mire'.

In the vicinity of Wilcebe Road there are no fewer than seven wells, each carrying a message from the laird, some blunt, some humorous, some inexplicable. Together, they lead you into a delightful corner of Glen Tanar which is well away from the main visitor areas.

The first well is at the car-park, where there is a water-trough opposite Braeloine Bridge. It carries the Gaelic inscription Ceud Mile Failte, wishing you 'A Hundred Thousand Welcomes'. Go through a gate behind the well and cross the car park track to a narrow path with

INFORMATION

Distance: 6 km (4 miles).

Start and finish: Braeloine Bridge car park, Glen Tanar. Take estate road from Bridge of Ess, about 2.5km west of Aboyne on B976.

Terrain: Good tracks or road all the way. No special footwear needed.

Refreshments: None en route.

Visitor Centre Braeloine Interpretive Centre is open daily in the summer.

One of the Wilcebe Road wells.

a sign pointing to 'Juniper Viewpoint'. Further up the path, another sign points rightward to the viewpoint, which looks down on the glen.

Back on the path, you go through a small gate and into a field where hill ponies sometimes graze. This leads to yet another gate, which opens onto a tarmac road running from Glen Tanar to the B976. It takes you past Belrorie House, where a giant sequoia tree towers up on the right of the road.

Another of the

Wilcebe Road wells.

The road passes a track to Hillhead Farm, and as you go downhill a superb view of the Dee Valley opens up on your right. Mighty Morven can be seen, and little Mullach Hill, crowned with Mullach's Cairn, traditionally marking the spot where a Danish king is said to have fallen; then there is Loch Kinord on the Muir of Dinnet, and in the distance the long ridge of Pressendye behind Tarland.

At a fork, a track leads off to the right. At the top of it you will see a huge rectangular stone, a granite memorial erected by the indefatigable Cunliffe Brooks. It carries the barely readable inscription 'Fir Munth. Ancient Pass over the Grampians. Here crossed the invading armies of Edward I of England AD 1296 and 1303. Also the army of Montrose 1645'. Some experts say the laird was wrong on all three counts! This track is your return route.

On your right at this fork, you will see the second well – Snakeswell. It got the name because its inscription read: 'The worm of the still is the deadliest snake on the hill', an obvious allusion to the illicit whisky distilling that went on around here. A semi-circular wall shelters it, with some of the stones acting as a seat for thirsty wayfarers.

At the fork is the sign 'Wilcebe Road'. Follow it to the left, passing Tillycairn Farm, and where the road bends right, set well back on the left and partly overgrown, is the third well. Unlike some of the other wells, this one is still giving out water. There is even a drinking cup attached to it. But if you use it, be careful - there's a hole in the cup! And take heed of what WCB had to say about it. The inscription on the well reads 'Well to know when you are Well off'.

The road turns right at Newton Farm (about 1.3km from the Wilcebe Road sign), and heads north-west. Watch for the entrance to a field on your left, set well back from the road and with a curious pile of twisted stones on the left-hand side of the gate. These are the kind of grotesque stones that Cunliffe Brooks used in different parts of the estate – you will see some on the dykes in Wilcebe Road.

The stones have been built around the fourth well,

A mare and its foal on the path to Wilcebe Road.

which has no running water. Its cryptic message reads 'Drink, Thank, Think'. What our eccentric laird expected us to think about will never be known, but perhaps it was the land around his wells, rich and fertile, stretching away to the Dee and the distant hills.

The road now goes down to Netherton Farm, where it turns right; at the corner two more giant sequoia trees stand guard on either side of the track. On the wall around one of the trees is that familiar sign – 'Wilcebe Road'.

But soon you leave Wilcebe Road. Go sharp left down to the B976 and turn right along this road. Two mysterious wells lie ahead. The fifth well is at Dinnet Bridge, but is almost inaccessible. It can be seen on the west (Dinnet) side of the river, at the foot of the nearest side of the bridge as you approach it. It is difficult to imagine why anyone should build a well only a few feet from the river. Even more inexplicable is the inscription – 'Alike yet so different'.

The next well, the sixth, is built into the dyke at Fasnadarroch House, about 500m from the bridge on your way towards Aboyne. Look for it on your left. The inscription says: 'The Well of Grace'. What romantic story lies behind that simple phrase?

The seventh and last well is the Daddy of them all – the most unusual, and some say the most unsightly. It was built into the wall of the old Glen Tanar School to celebrate the Jubilee of Queen Victoria, 'a bright and shining light to her people'. The well carries a number of Cunliffe Brooks' inscriptions. One, which appears beside one of WCB's mis-shapen stones, seems to be directed at square pegs in round holes. 'Shape thyself for use', it reads. 'the stone that may fit in the wall is not left in thy way'.

Across the road from the well is the Firmounth track, which is signposted. Follow it past the cottage called Gean Brae and turn off on a track on the right. This is the track that leads to the Edward I stone, and from there down Belrorie Hill to the car park. You are back where you started – at the end of the Seven Wells walk.

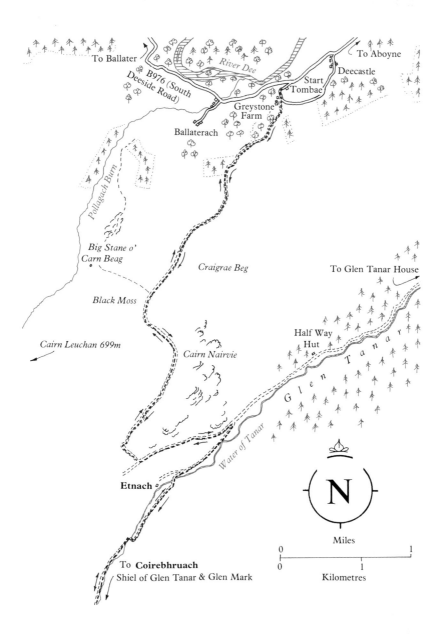

To Ballater

River Dee

To Aboyne

B976 (South Deeside Road)

Deecastle

Start
Tombae

Greystone
Farm

Ballaterach

Pollagach Burn

*Big Stane o'
Carn Beag*

Craigrae Beg

To Glen Tanar House

Black Moss

Cairn Leuchan 699m

Half Way
Hut

Cairn Nairvie

Glen Tanar

Water of Tanar

Etnach

N

Miles

0   1

To **Coirebhruach**
Shiel of Glen Tanar & Glen Mark

0   1

Kilometres

ETNACH AND COIREBHRUACH

We'll up the moor of Charlestown
And o'er the water of Dee,
And hine away to Candecaill,
It's there that we should be.

That verse from an old song points the way to what was once one of the most important Mounth passes from Deeside to the south; it went, according to a 17th century list of routes from the River Dee to the River Tay, 'from Canakyle to Innermarkie'. Innermarkie was Invermark in Glen Esk, Charlestown was Aboyne, and Candedail or Canakyle was what is now known as Deecastle, four miles east of Ballater on the South Deeside Road (B976).

The name Canakyle has changed over the years, but the correct version is believed to be Ceann-na-Coille, meaning Woodhead or Woodend. It was here on the south side of the Dee that the first Marquis of Huntly built Dee Castle, which became the principal residence of his family, but it was accidentally burned to the ground in 1641. Some years later it was replaced by a shooting lodge.

Although the Mounth road has long since slipped into disuse, you can still follow this ancient route through the Glentanar hills to Mount Keen and Glenesk. The starting point is Tombae, a little west of Deecastle. From here the road goes up past the farm of Greystone, whose farmhouse is built in the distinctive style introduced by Sir William Cunliffe Brooks when he was laird of Glen Tanar. Some people complained that he was bringing an English oast-house style to Scotland.

The rough track from Greystone clears the woods and pushes up the west side of Craigrae Beg. It is a long, steady climb, but not too demanding. On the right as you climb are the peaty acres of the Black Moss, stretching away to Cairn Leuchan. Here and there, grouse come squawking out of the heather. The Institute of Terrestrial Ecology at Banchory carries out grouse research on these moors. On the brow of the

INFORMATION

Distance: 11 km (7 miles) to Etnach and back. Add 5 km (3 miles) for Coirebhruach.

Start and finish: Tombae, about halfway between Aboyne and Ballater on the B976. Park in unofficial layby a few hundred metres west of Tombae (towards Ballater).

Terrain: Good track all the way, no steep climbs. Boots or strong shoes needed.

Refreshments: None en route. Wide choice in Aboyne and Ballater.

Looking down on Etnach from the hill above the farm.

hill the way is barred by a gate and fence. On the other side, as a stone-mounted information panel indicates, you are in the National Nature Reserve of Glen Tanar.

The track here becomes rougher as it swings round Cairn Nairvie (the name means 'the hill of the dyke'), finally heading downhill towards the Water of Tanar. Ahead, the green grass of Etnach begins to appear. The track turns left where a line of shooting butts crosses the heather, heading down to the Glen Tanar track. Some outbuildings come into view on the higher slopes of Etnach, then the old keeper's house can be seen nestling on the edge of the Tanar. Behind it, river and road chase each other uphill towards Coirebhruach at the head of the glen.

Etnach from the main Glen Tanar road to Mount Keen.

The ghost of Queen Victoria will keep you company here. This was the route she took when returning to Balmoral from one of her Great Expeditions. 'Eatnoch', was how she entered it in her diary. When the Queen was there in 1861 the only person to be seen was 'a wretched idiot girl', who sat on the ground 'with her hands round her knees, rocking herself to and fro and laughing'. She was blissfully unaware that she was in the presence of royalty.

It is hard to believe that great bellowing herds of cattle once stirred the dust on this remote pass from Deecastle to Etnach – 'a lonely place', Queen Victoria called it – and even today, with hill-walkers tramping through Glen Tanar, it still seems isolated from the outside world. This was the way the drovers came in their long trek to the trysts in the south, down from Strathdon and Gairnside, over the Dee and 'hine away to Candecaill'. They halted at Etnach for the night before pushing on to Coirebhruach at the head of Glen Tanar.

Etnach is about five miles from Glen Tanar House. Walkers deciding to skip the return journey to Greystone can arrange to be picked up at the car park near the estate buildings. But your route lies in the opposite direction, turning right at Etnach, past a sturdy stone bridge spanning the Tanar and on to Coirebhruach. This was another drovers' stop, for in the days of the great cattle drives there was an inn at Coirebhruach, serving thirsty travellers making the giant 'leap-frog' over Mount Keen to Glenmark. A rickle of stones is all that remains of the inn.

A few hundred yards from Coirebhruach, up the Tanar, there is another, more recent ruin – the burned-out shell of the Shiel of Glentanar, once a shooting lodge, where many a weary traveller found shelter when the winds came howling off Mount Keen. At one time there was a graffiti scribble on a wall saying that one George Sutherland had stabled his horse there in 1890. He was back in 1922, 'enjoying a picnic', but this time he came by car.

Looking up the Water of Tanar to Etnach.

Coirebhruach is the turn-around point on this walk, taking you back by Etnach to Tombae. On the way there, look for two fading tracks just past the gate at the Glen Tanar boundary. The second track goes off to the Pollagach Burn, where the Ordnance Survey map shows a rocking stone on the east bank.

Henry Alexander, later Sir Henry, Lord Provost of Aberdeen and author of the classic book *The Cairngorms*, saw the same map entry back in the 1920s and went in search of the rocking stone. It was first recorded by the Ordnance Survey in 1865 and was known locally as the Big Stone of Carn Beag. Nowadays, it is impossible to get even the slightest movement out of it. Perhaps young Geordie Byron did better. It was up by the Pollagach Burn that the young poet came when he spent his holidays at Ballaterach, wandering across the grey-brown moors and looking across the Dee to the 'dark Lochnagar' that he was later to write about so memorably.

Ballaterach is only a short distance from Greystone Farm. Isaac Stephen, a carpenter, had a workshop at Greystone and the young Byron was always nosing about the place. He was, said Isaac, 'an ill-tricket nickum' – a mischievous lad. Isaac's daughter, Mrs Calder, who was married to the farmer at Greystone, described Byron as 'a very takkin laddie, but nae easily managed'.

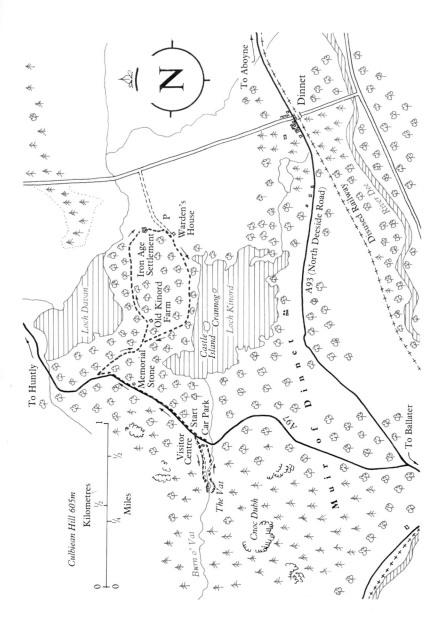

To Aboyne

Dinnet

River Dee

Disused Railway

A93 (North Deeside Road)

Loch Davan

Warden's House

P

Iron Age Settlement

Old Kinord Farm

Loch Kinord

Castle Island

Crannog

Memorial Stone

M u i r   o f   D i n n e t

A97

To Huntly

Start

Car Park

Visitor Centre

The Vat

Burn o' Vat

Cnoc Dubh

To Ballater

Culbiean Hill 605m.

Kilometres

1   ½   ½   ¼

Miles

0   0

MUIR OF DINNET

The Muir of Dinnet is a National Nature Reserve covering 1520 hectares of undulating heath, glorious with purple heather in late summer, and crowned by the twin lochs of Kinord and Davan. Culblean Hill slopes down to the western shores of the two lochs. From it a turbulent burn feeds Loch Kinord after passing through one of Deeside's most spectacular attractions – the Vat.

Burn o' Vat is the starting point for a two-in-one walk which includes the Vat and takes you on a circular tour of the Muir. Before setting off, it is worth calling in at the Visitor Centre to find out more about the area. There is information on the vast range of wildlife (everything from microscopic water life to red deer and including 150 different kinds of birds and over 400 moths).

The first part of the walk starts at a sign, 'The Vat', on the edge of a wood behind the Centre. Follow the sign and go through the wood to the Vat Burn, which is crossed by stepping stones. Once over the stones, the route climbs up a lovely little glen where orchids can be seen in summer. It passes a wooden walkway on the right and comes to a dead-end at what seems to be an impenetrable rock barrier. Here you will see the burn tumbling through a narrow gap in the rocks – the entrance to the Vat.

To enter it you have to clamber over large rocks and pick your way up the burn over stones leading to the entrance. Take care – one slip and you will get your feet wet! Inside the Vat you will find yourself in a huge bowl-like cavern. Ringed with high rock and narrowly open to the sky, this giant pothole was formed after the last Ice Age. The burn running into it pours through a spectacular gorge between Cnoc Dubh and Culblean Hill.

It is an impressive sight. The Vat itself must have sheltered many a fugitive, but the most famous was a freebooter called Gilderoy MacGregor, who is said to have hidden behind a waterfall with just enough room to hold a man. Gilderoy was captured and hanged in 1658.

INFORMATION

Distance: From Burn o'Vat across Muir, 4 km (2.5 miles). Vat walk and walkway, 1.5 km (1 miles). Total length 5.5 km (3.5 miles).

Start and finish: Burn o'Vat. Take A93 and between Aboyne and Ballater, turn off onto A97 (signed to Huntly). Burn o'Vat is reached in just over 1.5 km.

Terrain: Easy walking on tracks and paths. Boots or wellies needed if you go into the Vat.

Refreshments: None en route.

Opening hours There is a Visitor Centre at the Burn o'Vat car park, open Mid-May to Sept, 10.00-18.00, closed Tuesday and Wednesday.

Burn o' Vat.

When you leave the Vat, go down the path and climb up the wooden walkway, which provides striking views of the Muir. There is also a special viewpoint which looks across Loch Kinord. The walkway ends at the car park where you started.

For the second stage of the walk, turn left at the car park and follow the A97 north towards Loch Davan. Watch out on the right for a parking area where there is a plaque commemorating the opening of the Reserve in 1977. There is another good view of Loch Kinord from here. Further along the road you pass a tall memorial stone, erected between Kinord and Davan in 1956 to mark the site of the Battle of Culblean. Fought in 1335, it was a turning-point in the Second War of Independence.

Burn o' Vat.

Still further on there is an opening on the right and a gate with an information board and map. Follow a good track going into the woods. Loch Davan can be seen through the trees on your left. Davan, which is less accessible than Kinord, is rich in birdlife. As may as 24,000 wintering geese have been seen on Davan, as well as mute and whooper swans. Stand on the road at the head of the loch as dusk falls on an October evening and you can watch the breathtaking spectacle of thousands of geese coming into land.

Where the track forks, go left. You will soon pass a ruined building on the right – all that remains of Old Kinord Farm. Beyond the ruin, a red gate leads into an attractive birchwood. Most of the trees are little more than 30 years old: one of the most important developments at the Reserve has been the recolonisation of birch.

The track leads to a road approaching the Reserve from Dinnet, but look for another track, not very distinct, which goes off to the right. This will take you to an Iron Age settlement, one of three prehistoric settlements going back 2,500–3,000 years. The one near New Kinord, which is the clearest and most accessible, consists of five circular enclosures that look like monster stone circles.

Leaving the settlement, continue on the track until it reaches the road from Dinnet. Turn right, past the warden's house and out into the open ground above Loch Kinord. In early summer, rafts of white water-lily and the rarer yellow lily lie on the surface.

Fishing on Loch Kinord.

There were three lochs on the Muir of Dinnet in prehistoric times, but one silted up and turned into a peat bog, which is still there today. Fishing is allowed on Loch Kinord, but only for pike, perch and eel. The favourite spot for fishing – and picnicking – is further up the loch. There is a rough path down to it from the track, but it is hidden in places by broom.

Not far offshore you will see a man-made island or 'crannog', built about 2,000 years ago. Long after these lake-dwellers had vanished, another island a little to the west – Castle Island – was turned into a medieval fortress. Malcolm Canmore, King of Scotland from 1058 to 1093, had a hunting lodge on it and Edward I is thought to have stayed there while his army camped on the moor. James IV spent a couple of nights in the castle in 1504.

It was said at one time that there had been eleven spellings of the name Kinord, and one of them was Canmore. Others included Kender, Ceander, Ceanmore and Kinnord. Before you leave the loch and climb back to the track, look for one final link with the past – a Pictish symbol stone, nearly two metres high and probably dating from the 9th century. It is fenced in and stands a little way above the loch, hidden by broom.

Not far from the Pictish stone, the track turns away from the loch, heading along a field on the right towards Davan. It passes the ruins of Old Kinord and links up with the route taken earlier, leading back to the A97. Turn left and retrace your steps down the road to the Burn o' Vat car park.

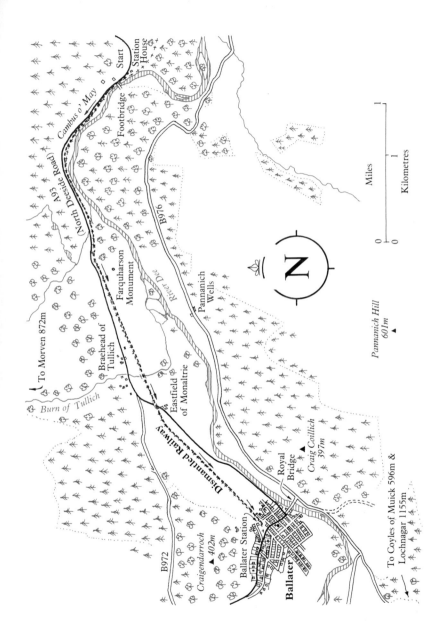

THE DEESIDE RAILWAY

A century ago, directors of the Great North of Scotland Railway Company held weekend board meetings in a saloon coach shunted into a siding at Cambus o' May station, near Ballater, when they had business to discuss. They knew what they were doing, for as they sat there talking about railway matters, and wining and dining in style, they found themselves looking out on one of the loveliest views on Deeside.

In those days, many people travelled from Aberdeen to Cambus o' May by train to picnic on the banks of the River Dee. Now the railway has gone and the trippers travel by car, but the old Royal line carries a different kind of traffic – walkers with packs on their backs. From Cambus o' May to Ballater the Deeside line has been turned into a walkway. Other sections of the old Aberdeen-Ballater railway have been opened to walkers, but none is as pleasant as the stretch of line where the Royal train once came puffing up from Cambus o' May on the last leg of its journey to Ballater.

The walk starts near the old platform, where the station building has now become Cambus Cottage. It has been turned into an attractive home, with an enviable view from the kitchen window. Walkers are kept away from it, for a small car park has been laid out just off the main road. Steps run down to the track and from there you set out past the long white span of Cambus o' May bridge. This was where the day trippers from Aberdeen swam and picnicked, and still do, below the bridge, which looks as good as it did when it was built in 1905. In fact, this bridge was built in 1984, and not in 1905, but it looks exactly like the original. When the old bridge was found to be badly in need of repair it was felt that it would be cheaper to build a new one, so the replacement went up at a cost of £80,000. It was opened by the Queen Mother in September 1988.

INFORMATION

Distance return:
13 km (8 miles).

Start: Cambus o'May, just off the A93 6.5km east of Ballater.

Finish: Ballater Station.

Terrain: Easy walking on a good surface. No special footwear needed.

Refreshments: Picnic site at Cambus 'May. Tearoom at Ballater Station, plus wide choice in Ballater itself.

Opening hours
Tourist Information Centre, Station Square, Ballater. Open Easter-October. Includes an exhibition on the old railway line.

Cambus o' May station.

Not far from the bridge, the path leaves the track and goes past a house known as Cutaway Cottage. This was an old wayside inn, and when the railway came to Ballater, it was so close to the line that one corner of it had to be cut off to allow the trains to pass. Curiously enough, it worked, but it must have rattled the crockery every time the 3.30 went up the Ballater line.

Beyond Cutaway Cottage, the path turns away from the river and rejoins the track, with birch trees forming a silver guard of honour on either side of the route. Wild roses bloom on the old line and, come June, the broom bursts out in all its golden splendour. As you walk, you can see the Dee curving round towards Cambus, a reminder of the meaning of the name – Cambus o' May, camas mhaigh, the Bend of the Plain. Some old spellings have it as Camas or Camus.

About 1.5 km west of the station a granite obelisk stands on top of a birch-clad knoll on the left. The monument, which can best be seen as you go further along the line from Cambus, was raised in memory of William Farquharson of Monaltrie, whose uncle, Francis Farquharson, fought at the head of the Farquharsons at Culloden in 1746. It was Francis who built an inn and developed Pannanich as a spa after 'miracle' waters were discovered there in 1760.

Pannanich, with its water, and Tullich, with its ancient kirkyard, glower at each other across the valley as if remembering the days when they competed for

Tullich kirkyard.

the crowds who came to Deeside for 'the cure'. If the cure didn't work, Tullich usually claimed the losers. The present Pannanich Wells Hotel can be seen across the Dee under Pannanich Hill. They still sell Pannanich water there, but no one claims that it has miraculous properties. They do say, however, that it is good for your health.

The ruined Kirk of Tullich, which is little more than a stone's throw from the walkway, is an ancient and fascinating place, with a picturesque circular wall and a valuable collection of Pictish sculptured stones. Tullich was a busy little hamlet at one time, with its own market cross, but when Pannanich blossomed and a new bridge was built over the Dee at Ballater, the community died. The famous Reel of Tullich is said to have originated there when kirk-goers were stamping their feet against the cold while waiting for their minister to turn up.

Past the kirkyard, a wooden bridge crosses the Burn of Tullich, which comes tumbling down from Byron's 'Morven of the Snows'. But other, less important hills lie ahead. Craig Coillich can be seen to the left, while between the rows of birch trees the pudding-bowl shape of Craigendarroch comes into view. Minutes later, the trees thin out and the track reaches Eastfield of Monaltrie.

The North Deeside Road, the A93, breaks the walkway at Eastfield. Across it, the track runs in a straight line to the station at Ballater. The last time a passenger train came whistling up this track was on Saturday 26th February 1966. From the walkway you can see in the distance the outline of the Coyles of Muick and, behind them, the great bulk of Lochnagar – a magnificent backcloth to the Royal Deeside town.

Looking over Ballater from Craigendarroch.

This last lap of your walk holds more memories than anywhere else on the Deeside line. As a plaque on the station wall says, Ballater Station was for over a century the scene of Royal arrivals and departures through six reigns from Queen Victoria in her 'Palace on Wheels' to Queen Elizabeth. The plaque commemorates the rebuilding of the station in 1886, when a Royal Waiting Room was opened for the Queen Victoria's use. The Royal loo is still there!

You can walk along the old line for a very short distance beyond the railway station, but it comes to an abrupt halt. Plans were made to carry the line on to Braemar, but Queen Victoria rejected the idea. Now the whole Royal line has gone and all that is left is a walkway where people can stroll in peace and enjoy the magnificent scenery.

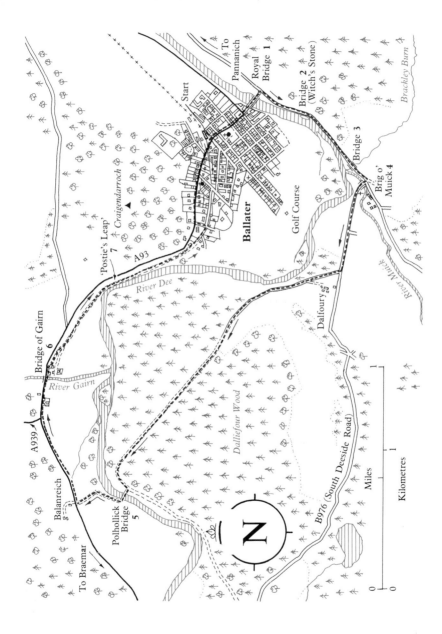

THE SEVEN BRIGS

Some lovely wooded countryside on Ballater's doorstep is the setting for the Seven Brigs Walk. It takes in three rivers and a handful of burns and it starts by walking from Station Square down to the Royal Bridge, which spans the Dee at the entrance to Ballater from the east.

Ballater has had three bridges on or near this site. The first was a stone bridge built about 100m east of the present bridge in 1783. It was swept away by floods in 1799 and a second stone bridge was built in 1809. The floods came again – the Muckle Spate of 1829 – and away went another bridge. When the first two arches collapsed, the splash of the water was so great that it rose over the tops of nearby houses. One half-drowned visitor who had come to Pannanich for its health-giving water said wryly, 'Call you this a watering-place?'

Next came a wooden bridge. That was in 1834 and it lasted until November 1885, when the present bridge was opened by Queen Victoria, who named it the Royal Bridge. Look over the east parapet wall and you will see the foundations of the 1834 timber bridge running in a line across the river.

Once over the bridge, turn right and go up the B976 road until you come to a high point in the road known as Spinnin' Jenny's. Jenny was a witch. A rock that stood at the roadside here was known as Spinnin' Jenny's Stane or the Witch's Stone. This is where you will find the second bridge. It has a low parapet on one side and is the least impressive of the seven.

Further on, two houses stand on either side of the road – Burnfoot and Bridgefoot. Just past them is bridge no 3, spanning the Brackley Burn before it meets the Dee.

Carry on until you come to the Bridgend of Muick, where a road goes off down Glen Muick. On its left you will see a memorial seat with a large plaque commemorating one of Queen Victoria's last public acts – taking the salute at a march past of Gordon Highlanders before they left for the Boer War in 1899. The Queen was by then getting frail, and she died in 1901, having reigned for 64 years.

INFORMATION

Distance: 7 km (4.5 miles).

Start and finish: Station Square, Ballater.

Terrain: Roads and good tracks. No special footwear needed.

Refreshments: Good choice in Ballater. Free parking in Station Square and Church Square; toilets in Church Square.

Opening hours Tourist Information Centre, Station Square (phone Ballater 55306), open daily Easter-Oct.

Queen Mother's fishing bothy.

The road from Ballater turns right at the Victoria Memorial and crosses the Brig o'Muick – the fourth bridge, built in 1858. On the west side of the bridge is Glenmuick Kirkyard, where faded tombstones tell of the people who lived in this corner of Deeside a century or more ago. Near the gate you will see a small coffin-shaped slab over the grave of John Mitchell. The dates on it, 1596 to 1722, show that he lived to the incredible age of 126.

He is said to have written a book in which he described how he was a bachelor for 40 years, married for 26 years, widowed for three years, and married again for 55 years. In the book was a poem with the lines:

> Between my cradle and my grave, I wean,
> Seven monarchs and a queen have been.

Mitchell, who was a skilful angler and a well-known poacher, lived at Dalfoury, not far from the Brig o'Muick, and along the route you will be taking. Having crossed the old bridge, follow the road - still the B976 – for about 800 m and then turn right onto a wide gravel track. From it, as you walk, you look across the Dee to Ballater, and across its golf course to the plum-pudding outline of Craigendarroch, the 'crag of the oaks'.

Now you are entering Daliefour Wood, a great pinewood that hugs the Dee to Polhollick Bridge and beyond. This is where John Mitchell lived, not far from the salmon that louped up the Dee and tempted him out with his rod.

Paths leave the main track and slip away to the river, and it is down one of these that another well-known figure has often been seen making her way to the fishing – the Queen Mother. Perhaps she plucked a seven-pounder from Mitchell's Red, a spawning ground for salmon, named after our old poaching friend.

One of her favourite fishing grounds was near Polhollick Bridge; another, in more recent years, was at a wooden fishing bothy built for her by the Royal Family on the banks of the Dee. Prince Charles sometimes fishes there too.

Polhollick Bridge is about 3 km from the Brig o' Muick. This long white suspension bridge was built in

1892 with money provided by a Ballater exile, Alexander Gordon from Kent, who also paid for the Cambus o' May bridge. Before the bridge was erected, there was a ferry at Polhollick, crossing a well-known angling pool known as the Boat Pool. The boathouse is still in use today as a dwelling-house.

Polhollick Bridge.

When you cross the Polhollick Bridge – bridge number five – a path takes you up to the A93 road, opposite the farm of Balanreich. Turn right towards Ballater and you will see a sign pointing across the road to steps leading up to a path which runs between the fields and the A93, well away from the traffic. It was laid out recently as a safety measure for walkers and it takes you back on to the main road near the sixth bridge – the Bridge of Gairn.

There have been three bridges over the Gairn, the first being a pack-bridge only a few feet wide. The second was built at the end of the 18th century, and the present bridge was erected in 1855. 'Not nearly as romantic-looking as the old bridge' wrote a local minister, the Rev James Crombie, and he was right.

But there is romance, and a tragic ending, at the seventh and final bridge. When you cross the Bridge of Gairn, look for a small path going down to the Auld Line. This was to have been the route of the Ballater to Braemar railway, but Queen Victoria put a stop to it, and now it is a favourite walk with both locals and visitors.

It runs parallel to the River Dee, passing through a small woodland. At one point the river bank steepens sharply, giving a nasty drop from the path, and as a safety measure a fence has been provided. From it you can look down on the Queen Mother's fishing bothy on the opposite bank of the Dee; who knows, you may even catch a glimpse of one of the Royal anglers.

On this high bank you will see a bridge spanning a wide ravine known as the 'Postie's Leap'. They say that when a lovelorn postman was jilted on the eve of his wedding, he walked along the Auld Line and jumped to his death from the last of the Seven Brigs.

The Auld Line runs for about 1.5 km from the Fit of Gairn, ending at a picnic spot on the banks of the Dee, next to the golf course. From there a path takes you on to the Braemar Road in Ballater, only a short distance from the centre of the village.

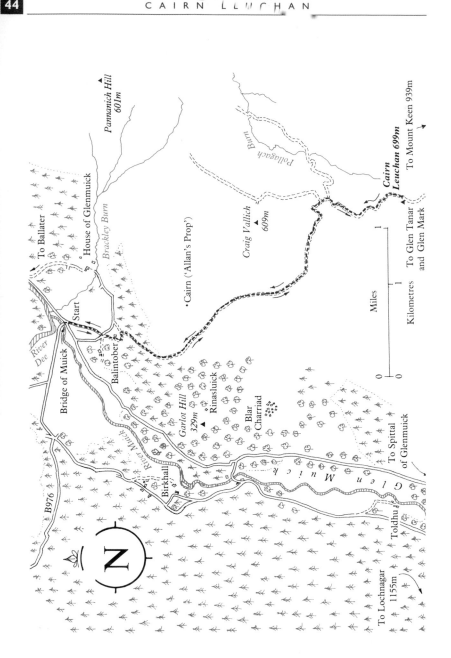

CAIRN LEUCHAN

The dusty tracks across the hills of Deeside were once vital links between busy communities. They went over the Mounth from Aboyne to Tarfside, from Braemar to Braedownie, from Glen Muick to Glen Clova. One of the most important routes was the Whisky Road, starting near Ballater and crossing the moors to Glen Tanar and Glen Mark.

To follow this old whisky trail, make your way to the Bridge of Muick, about 1.5 km from Ballater on the South Deeside Road (B976). Here you will see a memorial marking the spot where Queen Victoria took the salute as the Gordon Highlanders marched off to the Boer War. To the left is a track with a sign marked 'Balintober'. This takes you up to the keeper's house at Balintober, well to the right of the House of Glenmuick. Just beyond Balintober the road swings right and climbs uphill to a deer fence. Go through the gate and you are on the edge of a vast expanse of moorland.

Below on the right is Glen Muick, and if you look hard enough as you make your way up the hill you will see an indistinct path coming up through the heather. It is a link with a 'lost' community, a scattering of ruined settlements hidden away from the cars that stream up the Glen Muick road on their way to the Spittal and the hills of Lochnagar. These settlements were scattered throughout the glen from Bridgend to the Spittal, or Spittelhauche as it was called in 1600. They had names like Bog, Rinasluick, Balnoe,

INFORMATION

Distance return:
10 km (6 miles).

Start and finish:
Bridge of Muick, 1.5 km from Ballater on B976. Limited parking space at bridge; alternatively, walk from Ballater or be dropped off at the Balintober road.

Terrain: Good track all the way; steady climb to Cairn Leuchan. Boots or strong shoes.

Refreshments: Wide choice in Ballater.

On top of Cairn Leuchan.

Byallachur, Toildow or Toldhu (the black hole), and Clashmuick (the pigs' furrow). On Garlot Hill, which you can see from the Balintober road, you can still pick out the lines of run-rig farming.

Perhaps the most interesting site is Blar Charriad. It was shown on an 1869 map as Balacariag, and it was said to be 'a substantial township of twelve houses, three enclosures and a corn-drying kiln'. The kiln is still there, and you feel as if you were walking through a recognisable township. It was linked to another settlement shown on the 1869 map as Loinmore, where there were five houses. The map also shows a track running across the moor from Loinmore to the hill road from Balintober – the road you are walking on. The heather has almost buried this link with the ruined settlements, but at one time there was a steady movement of people and cattle going south over the hills.

The name Blar Charriad means 'field of conflicts'. It may be that one of the conflicts involved John Farquharson of Inverey, the Black Colonel, who featured in the ballad, The Baron of Blaickley. Farquharson slew John Gordon of Brackley in a 'battle' that took place in these hills. Braichlie or Braikley House stood on the site of the present House of Glenmuick.

As you go up the hill towards the Pollogach Burn – the Pollach road, it was called – a prominent cairn can seen on the left. This is known as Allan's Prop (a prop is a landmark), named after a previous owner of the estate, Sir Allan Mackenzie. Beyond the cairn is Craig Vallich, where the road swings left and goes on up to the ridge. It is a long, steady slog to the top, but take it easy and look about you - the views are outstanding. Three paths meet on the ridge. One goes to Pannanich Hill, the other crosses the Pollogach Moss to Glen Tanar. Queen Victoria wrote about riding over this sodden peat moss, adding, 'We avoided getting into any of the bogs'. Sensible woman that she was, she stayed on her pony while crossing what she called this 'soft bit'.

Your way is by the third path on the right. It climbs up to a rock formation called Cairn Leuchan, which from below, silhouetted again st the sky, looks like some mysterious fairy castle. The climb to the top is well worth it. From it you look down into the valley of the Muick, with the Birkhall road winding its way towards Lochnagar. You can see the path that clears the woods at Allt-na-guibhsaich and rises steeply towards the 'frowning glories' of Byron's mountain.

Turning round, you look into the face of Mount Keen, the old Mounth track a hairline mark against its great cone. The track goes over the west shoulder of the hill some 180m below the summit. At 938m (3077 ft), this is the most easterly Munro in Scotland, and it dominates the Dee valley. Up there, mountain hares flee at your coming, their summer-brown coats changing to winter white late in the season, and hawks hover overhead, preparing to dive on their unsuspecting prey. Deer can be seen watching warily from a long way off.

Clouds over the Deeside hills.

Cairn Leuchan is the turning-point of the walk, but it is worthwhile going farther along the track so that you can drink in the scenery down in Glen Muick. There are other tracks that take you down into the glen, but car arrangements would have to be made if you were planning to do this. So it's back by the 'fairy castle' and down to Balintober. Before you leave Cairn Leuchan, look away to the north-east and you will see two lochs in the distance. These are Loch Kinord and Loch Davan, whose waters lie like giant dewdrops on the Muir of Dinnet.

There is a wonderful sense of peace and isolation in the moors between Glen Muick and Glen Tanar. It will leave you wanting more.

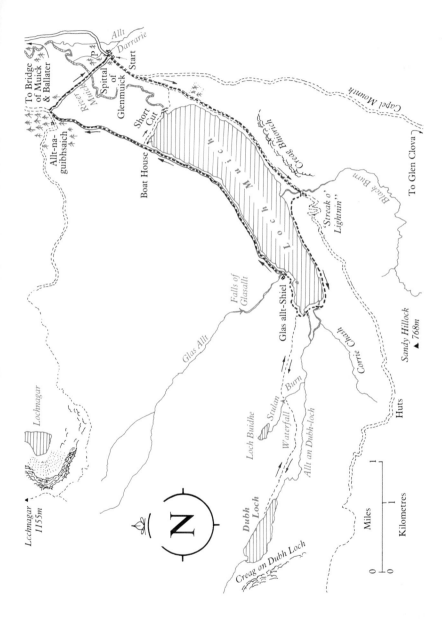

LOCH MUICK CIRCUIT

When Queen Victoria came to Balmoral last century there were no Royal lodges at Loch Muick, no motor cars, and no tourists. Even then, however, there were signs that hill-walkers and climbers were beginning to make forays into the Deeside hills, for in 1892 the Queen proposed that there should be 'a closed time of six weeks against tourists'.

Happily, nobody took up her suggestion, and in 1974 a different Royal attitude was shown when Balmoral estate and the Scottish Wildlife Trust set up the the Glen Muick and Lochnagar Wildlife Reserve. So today, as another century draws to a close, hundreds of tourists head for Glen Muick in the summer months. For them, Loch Muick is one of the main attractions – the jewel in the Balmoral crown. This lovely stretch of water, 3 km long, has become a firm favourite with walkers, and those with staying power can extend the Loch Muick Circuit by tramping another 3km to the Dubh Loch.

From the Spittal of Glenmuick car park, cross the bridge over the Allt Darrarie and go down to the Visitor Centre, which will tell you all you want to know about the area, including the weather and temperature. Outside, a telescope gives you a close-up view of red deer on Creag na Slabhraidh, behind the car park. Winter is the best time to see the deer. Driven down from the high tops by the cold and snow, they can be seen foraging for food around the Spittal buildings. They are fed by the Balmoral keepers and at this time of the year their fear of human beings is less urgent than their need to stave off starvation.

INFORMATION

Distance: 11 km (7 miles). Add a further 8 km (5 miles) for Dubh Loch.

Start and finish: Spittal of Glenmuick. Take B976 from Ballater to Bridge of Muick and turn left on the Glen Muick road. The Spittal is reached in 11 km. This is a narrow road, unsuitable for caravans. Please drive with care. Toilets at the Spittal car park.

Terrain: Good track for most of the way; narrow path on the east side of the loch. Boots and waterproofs recommended.

Refreshments: None. Take food and drink with you.

Opening hours There is a small Visitor Centre at Spittal of Glenmuick, run by the Scottish Wildlife Trust, and open in the summer months. A ranger may be present. The Centre has information on the terrain and wildlife of the area, and the latest weather forecast is usually posted on the wall.

Walkers heading for Loch Muick.

A large key hangs on display in the window of the Visitor Centre. This was the key to the old hospice, or Spittal, that sheltered drovers and other travellers going over the Capel Mounth on their way south. The hospice stood where the track to the loch meets the track to Lochnagar. Take the route to the loch, keeping right where the the Capel heads left, and walk towards a small woodland on the left.

The Capel was a major route to Glen Clova and the south. The Jacobites, the drovers, the thravers – this ancient mountain pass has seen them all. It was probably the first hill track to be churned up by bicycles, although mountain bikes had not been heard of when it happened. That was on a May day in 1892, when 16 cyclists went pedalling up the hill, the first to cross from Glenmuick to Glen Clova.

Reflections on Loch Muick.

While the Capel climbs out of sight, your track runs on above the loch, under the rising slopes of Creag Bhiorach, with the surrounding hills mirrored in its placid waters. Loch Muick, which falls to a depth of 80m, had good trout fishing at one time, although the trout were small. Two boats were used on the loch by Royal anglers before the war, one for carrying people up the loch, the other for fishing. Pre-war photographs show King George V and the Duke of York (later King George VI) making a sweep with a net to augment their catch.

Because of its altitude and exposure, Loch Muick attracts few birds, but with luck you may see goosanders flying to and from the loch along the line of the river. A pair of red-throated divers have spent the summer on the loch in recent years, but there have been no reports of breeding. Three kilometres from the Spittal is the Black Burn, whose peaty waters come frothing down into a lovely little bay. The burn is crossed by a wooden bridge. On the other side a rough track rises steeply up to the plateau, but your route is to the right, where a signpost points to the Loch Muick Circuit. A narrow footpath, stony and awkward in places, clings to the hill slope as it follows the loch to its sandy south-west beach.

Winter on Loch Muick.

Where the path turns across the head of the loch you pass another path which climbs steeply up by Corrie Chash to the Sandy Hillock Huts. Some people call this the Streak of Lightning, and seen from the loch it certainly looks like that, but, in fact, the name was originally given to the bulldozed track, formerly a zig-zag path, which climbs up from the Black Burn.

A stream called the Allt an Dubh-loch, which feeds Loch Muick, is bridged at various points as you cross the head of the loch to to the Glas allt-Shiel track. Here, a path goes left to the Dubh Loch. For those who want to go to the Dubh Loch the following brief information may be useful:

The Dubh Loch (black loch) is 3 km from Loch Muick, a little further if you go to the head of it. The

Reflections on Loch Muick.

path is very narrow in places and care has to be taken. At the loch itself the ground can be wet and boggy. The path climbs about 250m. On the right, half-way up, the Stulan Burn comes tumbling down from Loch Buidhe. Near the Stulan waterall there is a cairn marking the spot where the Marquess of Lorne proposed to Princess Louise on 3rd October 1870. Climbers are drawn to the Dubh Loch by the cliff face known as Creag an Dubh Loch. Some of Britain's top climbers have trained here before tackling Alpine or Himalayan peaks. Some walkers use the Dubh Loch as a route to get to the summit of Lochnagar.

If you are not taking in the Dubh Loch on your walk, follow the path from the head of the loch towards the woods at Glas allt-Shiel . This granite lodge – the 'shiel of the grey burn' - stands on a pine-covered delta and takes its name from a stream which drops down the steep slope behind it. It is a romantic spot, and at one time rhododendrons bloomed there. They have now been removed, leaving the shiel open to the eyes of Royal watchers on the other side of the loch. It was a favourite picnic spot of Queen Victoria and Prince Albert and the Queen built the shiel after Prince Albert's death. She called it her 'Widow's House'.

There is a by-pass path which, as well as keeping you away from the Royal front door, takes you through the woods to a narrow path leading up to Lochnagar by

Loch Muick from the Capel Mounth, with Glas-allt-Shiel on the right.

the Falls of Glas-allt, which are well worth seeing. The Shiel is still used by members of the Royal Family and their house parties. The bypass takes you back on to a good track, which runs up the edge of the loch. In about 3 km you reach an old boathouse. At one time it housed a speedboat which the Duke of Edinburgh used on the loch, but nothing like that happens to-day. The shores would be black with spectators if it did. From the boathouse a path provides a short cut across the end of the loch and over a footbridge crossing the River Muick to the Spittal track.

Ignoring the short-cut, carry on for about 2 km until Allt-na-giubhsaich (stream of the pines) is reached. This pine-sheltered lodge, fronted by yew trees and bright with rhododendrons early in the summer, looks out to Loch Muick. It was a sod-covered, one-chimney building at the beginning of the 19th century, but by the time Victoria and Albert purchased Balmoral it had become 'a most commodious cottage'. The Queen called it her 'Hut'. King George VI spent a month here recovering from whooping cough when he was a boy.

Beyond Allt-na-giubhsaich, turn right on the track back to the Spittal. In the fields to the right – and occasionally in the woods near the Visitor Centre – deer can often be seen, but as the season moves on and visitors begin to arrive, they shake off their winter ties with the Spittal and head for the high tops.

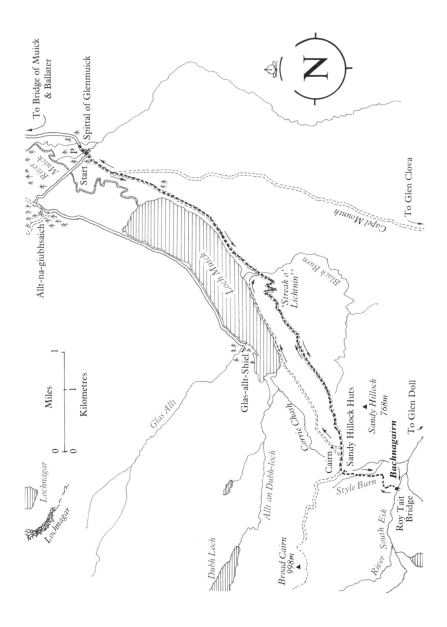

BACHNAGAIRN

The cleughs o' Bachnagairn' are at the end of this walk – a land 'where water rins and gowans blaw, and Grampian mountains busk their heids wi' snaw.' It is one of the more spectacular ways to cross the Grampians and it offers an alternative to the route by the Capel Mounth to Glen Clova.

As in the Loch Muick Circuit (walk 12), the starting point is the Spittal of Glenmuick. For the first 3 km you follow the track along the east shore of the loch to the Black Burn. Cross the bridge, and then go left up a broad, bulldozed track to the plateau. This was formerly a zig-zag path known as the Streak o' Lichtnin (Streak of Lightning) and even now it is a hard push – so take it slowly. Once on top, the track runs south-west, keeping to the edge of the high ground above the loch.

Up there, beside a cairn at the top of the lightning streak, you have an eagle's-eye view of Glen Muick . . . the road coming down from Allt na-Guibhsaich, the dark cleft of the Dubh Loch path, the hills throwing their reflections into Loch Muick, and Glas-allt Shiel, where you may see tiny figures moving about the delta and wonder if the Royals are at Balmoral. From here, too, you will get a glimpse of a narrow path dropping steeply down Corrie Chash to the head of Loch Muick. This is the way you will return to the Spittal.

Bare moorland, riddled with peat hags, stretches out on your left as you continue along the track above what are known as the Loch Braes. The track bears gently away from the Braes and just under 3 km from the cairn on top of the zig-zag you come upon a corrugated-iron stable and bothy known as the Sandy Hillock Huts. In recent years they replaced two small ramshackle cabins built in the days before Land-Rovers churned up the hills. When a Royal shooting party was out on the moors, hill ponies were tethered at the Huts until needed to carry the dead deer downhill. Today, the huts are still used by soldiers on ponies, armed with walkie-talkies, who patrol the area when Prince Charles is out with the guns.

INFORMATION

Distance return:
16 km (10 miles).

Start and finish:
Spittal of Glenmuick. From Ballater take B976 to Bridge of Muick, and fork left onto the Glen Muick road. The road ends at the Spittal car park in 11km. This is a narrow road, unsuitable for caravans. Please drive with care. Toilets at the car park.

Terrain: Good track to Sandy Hillock huts, then narrow downhill path to Bachnagairn. Boots and good water-proofs essential. OS Landranger map sheet 44 and a compass should be carried. This walk should not be attempted by inexperienced walkers in poor weather conditions.

Refreshments: None. Take adequate food and drink with you.

Visitor Centre
There is a small Visitor Centre at Spittal of Glenmuick, run by the Scottish Wildlife Trust. It is open daily in the summer months, and there may be a ranger present. The Centre has information on the terrain and wildlife of the area and the latest weather forecast is usually posted on the wall.

The Huts mark a mountain junction. Before reaching them, you will see a triangle of grass on the right where two narrow paths converge and go down to Loch Muick by Corrie Chash. There is a small cairn where the paths meet.

Beyond the Huts, the main track bears slightly right and goes on to Broad Cairn. If you want to 'bag' a Munro, Broad Cairn, whose summit is about 3 km from the Huts, is a straightforward climb. But your route is down, not up, following a path that turns left just beyond the Huts and goes south beside the Style Burn to Bachnagairn. Other small paths at the Sandy Hillock Huts run into the heather and fade away, so make sure you are on the Bachnagairn path – follow the line of the fence behind the Huts.

Climbing up from Loch Muick on the way to Bachnagairn.

This narrow path drops towards the trough of the South Esk. Now you are really in the land 'where water rins and gowans (mountain daisies) blaw.' It is an idyllic spot. Dorothy Maria Ogilvy of Clova, an Angus poet, dipped into a rich broth of local dialect last century and painted a vivid picture of the the 'yammering yearn' (eagle) rising above the 'cleughs' (ravines) of Bachnagairn, seeking his 'wild wonnying' (dwelling place) on 'bauld Braidcairn'.

The downward path is fairly steep in places and in wet weather it can be slippery, so care is needed. Bachnagairn unveils its beauty slowly. First you see the fringe of the Bachnagairn firs, the slope of the hills east of the Tolmount pass, and, away to the left, the dark knuckle of Glen Doll. In this tree-lined setting of lofty crags and cascading waterfalls, the infant River Esk acts as an unofficial boundary between Deeside and Angus.

People come up from Glen Clova to picnic on this spot, crossing the bridge that spans the Esk. There is a sad, yet inspiring story about the bridge. When an Aberdeen man, Roy Tait, was killed on Lochnagar, his friends in Dundee, where he worked, decided to build a memorial to him – a bridge to replace a structure that was in poor repair. For months they worked on the project, taking beams and other heavy material partly up the hill by tractor, then carrying it the rest of the way on their backs. Now you cross the Roy Tait bridge when you step from Deeside to Angus. On the

Clova side, you will see a plaque which says that the bridge was built by Roy Tait's family and friends and that he died on Lochnagar in August 1981.

A long strip of woodland drapes the banks of the river as it rushes down from Loch Esk, which is about a mile from the bridge. At Bachnagairn it drops about 20m in one great leap, through a ravine obscured by overhanging trees. Track and river chase each other down to the broad Clova valley, passing the point where the Capel Mounth comes in.

The bridge at Bachnagairn.

Some people make the circuit from Loch Muick by Bachnagairn and back by the Capel to the Spittal of Glenmuick. That is a long, hard trail and not for us, but it is still worth crossing to the Angus side to explore Bachnagairn. Like Dorothea Maria, you may see 'whaaps (curlews), white hares, hoody craws and ptarmigan'. And wild flowers. The South Esk at Bachnagairn is a botanist's paradise.

Bachnagairn wasn't always deserted. There was once a shooting lodge there owned by Sir Alan Russell Mackenzie, 2nd Baronet in Glenmuick, and two fragments of a wall and the corner of a fireplace are buried in the grass about 100m from the bridge. The ruins of the stables are on the other side of the path.

So, no doubt reluctantly, you leave Bachnagairn and its magnificent setting and climb back to where Dorothy Maria could 'feel the wuns blaw frae the Capel Mount'. Beyond the Sandy Hillock Huts, look for a path going off through a rocky area on the left. This is one of the two paths mentioned earlier, converging and going down to the head of Loch Muick.

Here you have to make a choice. The Corrie Chash route opens up a superb view of Loch Muick, but it is sandy, very steep, tricky in places, and can be hazardous in wet weather. The name means 'corrie of the difficulty', and that description could apply to the path as well as to the corrie itself, so considerable care has to be taken. You have to decide if you want to go back this way or to stick by the easier zig-zag route down the track to the Black Burn.

Either way, the last lap of the walk is along the east shore of Loch Muick, back to the Spittal.

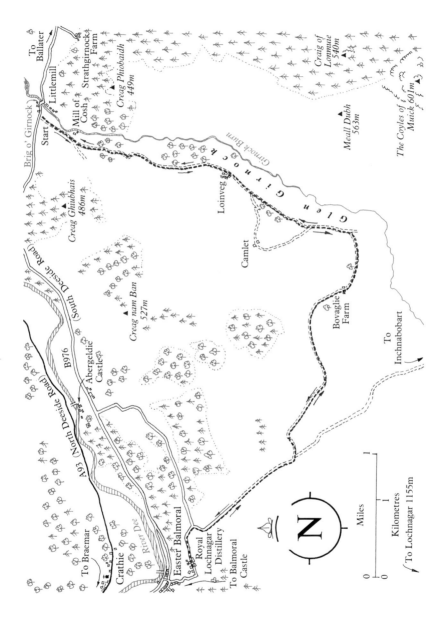

GLEN GIRNOCK

Whisky-smugglers and witches will be on your heels on this walk. The starting point is Littlemill, 5 km west of Ballater, where the B976 does a sharp double twist over the Brig o' Girnock on its way to Balmoral. This lovely little hamlet, disturbed only by traffic avoiding the North Deeside Road (the Royal Family use it as an 'escape route' from Balmoral) is at the mouth of Glen Girnock, or Strathgirnock as it is sometimes called. There is a farm of Strathgirnock about 1km east of Littlemill. The glen lies between two wooded hills called Creag Phiobaidh (piper's crag) and Creag Ghiubhais (pine crag), and the way into it from your parking place is by a track that follows the line of the Girnock Burn, passing an old mill on the left and a scattering of houses on the right.

It is a peaceful glen, yet it has had a curiously violent past. One of the most tragic feuds of the 16th century had its roots in Strathgirnock. The Forbes of Strathgirnock and the Gordons of Knock had an undying hatred of each other. It reached a terrible climax when Alexander Forbes slew Francis Gordon, who wanted to marry his daughter. He later

INFORMATION

Distance return:
16 km (10 miles) to Easter Balmoral. The walk may be shortened by turning back at Bovaglie Farm, which makes it a 9 km (6 miles) round trip.

Start: Littlemill. Take the B976 west from Ballater. Littlemill is reached in about 5 km, and you park in the trees near the bridge. If walking to Easter Balmoral, you will have to arrange to be collected.

Terrain: Good track all the way. Strong shoes advised.

Refreshments: None en route. Tearoom at Royal Lochnagar Distillery.

Opening hours
Royal Lochnagar Distillery: Easter-Oct, Mon-Sat 10.00-17.00, Sun 11.00-16.00. Nov-Mar, Mon-Fri 10.00-17.00. Visitor Centre, tearoom, guided tours and whisky tasting.

Prince Charles's shiel at Inchnabobart, reached from Glen Girnock.

slaughtered Francis' seven brothers while they were cutting peat, then stuck their heads on their flaughter spades (peat-cutting spades). Forbes paid for the killings with his own life; he was tracked down and hanged on a tree in Strathgirnock.

On Craig nam Ban, the Witch's Hill – Lochnagar in background.

When you clear the woods at Littlemill, the track runs past the foot of a hill called Creag nam Ban (the hill of the women), on the right. Here is another reminder of Strathgirnock's gory past. Witches were burned on the summit of the hill, the most famous of them being Kitty Rankine, 'French Kate', a maid at Abergeldie Castle. Whether or not the stories about her Black Magic are true is anybody's guess, but George VI stayed at Abergeldie Castle and his brother Bertie (later, briefly, Edward VIII) thought that its bat-infested tower was haunted by Kitty Rankine's ghost. There is a post on top of Creag nam Ban which is supposed to be the stake where she was burned – and they say her screams can still be heard on dark winter nights.

It is a pity that Creag nam Ban has such a murky reputation, for it is a lovely hill, wooded in places. Half-way along its summit there is a group of trees known as Jane's Firs, named after a woman who threw fir seeds away there after the estate refused to give her the price she wanted for them. There are also cairns scattered about the top of the hill, including one in memory of Queen Victoria's mother, the Duchess of Kent. The cairn was erected after her death in 1861.

For those want to climb the hill, the best approach is from a back road branching off the B976 near Abergeldie Castle. It can also be climbed from a number of points on the track from Littlemill – the route of this walk – the easiest and best place being at the deserted farm of Camlet. Incidentally, look out for an old lime kiln at the roadside near Camlet; it is in superb condition.

As you walk you will find that Strathgirnock, like so many other Deeside glens, carries the scars of depopulation, and Camlet is one of a number of abandoned farms. The first is Loinveg, about 2.5 km from Littlemill, and Camlet is a kilometre further on. Its name comes from An Cam-leathad, meaning 'the curved slope', which is not a bad description.

The farm sits well off the main route, at the top of a track that climbs up the hill from the glen road, then curves back to it in a great loop. The folk who lived at Camlet, cradled in the lap of Creag nam Ban, must have looked across the moors that stretched endlessly in front of them and felt that they were 'out of the world'. The rocky hill immediately above the farm is Sgor na h-Iolaire, the peak of the eagle, but you will not see eagles there now.

Ahead, as you push up the glen, Lochnagar comes into sight, and away to the left you can see the distinctive grass-covered slopes of the Coyles of Muick. The word Coyle comes from choille, meaning a wood, and these 'Coyles' are on the edge of a forest spreading up from Glen Muick. There is, in fact, only one Coyle, the highest of three hilltops which stand out against the skyline, but the name has come to be used collectively for the group. The other hills are Meall Dubh and the Craig of Loinmuie. The Coyles are part of a great belt of serpentine rock which runs south-westward from the Moray Firth through Deeside into Perthshire.

Just over a kilometre from Camlet a smaller track branches left to the Girnock Burn, while the main track swings right towards the woods of Bovaglie. The shuttered windows of Bovaglie Farm tell the same old story. What was once a busy 'ferm toun' is dead and deserted. The great Strathspey musician, J. Scott Skinner, wrote a tune called Bovaglie's Plaid, inspired, it seemed, by a local saying that the wood 'haps (shelters) Bovaglie ferm like a plaid'. No longer. The 'plaid' is ragged now, bruised by the winds that whip across the featureless moors around it. This is the turning point if you wish to walk back to Littlemill.

Deer are often seen sheltering in Bovaglie Wood. On your way through the wood, keep an eye open for a telephone pole on the right of the track with part of its trunk thinned down like a swan's neck. The thinning was done by deer rubbing their antlers on the pole when casting. The same thing can be seen on posts and power supply poles. With a little more antler scraping the Bovaglie pole would have snapped in two, but wire wrapped tightly around it put an end to the deer rubbing.

Bovaglia.

In winter and spring you may see herds of deer being fed by the Balmoral keepers, who leave carts of potatoes at the side of the track. Even more interesting is the 'call to lunch'. The keeper's Land Rover horn is the deers' dinner gong. You can hear it blasting across the moors and see the deer come running for their feed as bales of hay are pitched out to them. In this way, estates keep the deer from wandering away in winter - and fatten them up for the kill later in the year.

One of the 'dining areas' for potatoes in Strathgirnock is near Bovaglie Farm, but if you come across deer being fed be careful about your approach. The deer have no fear of keepers in winter, but they will take to their heels at the sight of strangers. From the farm the track slopes up to join another track, where you go right to Easter Balmoral and the Royal Lochnagar

Distillery. The left fork leads to Inchnabobart, once a small, remote farm near a ford across the River Muick, now a Royal lodge often used by Prince Charles.

Glen Girnock was notorious for its illegal whisky-making. There were no fewer than a dozen 'black bothies' (illicit stills) in the upper part of this small glen. It is said that the remains of old stills can still be found in the glen, but if you really want to see what a 'black bothy' looks like, the answer lies at Easter Balmoral, 3km away.

They don't turn out illicit whisky at Lochnagar Distillery, but at the back of the distillery they have constructed a 'black bothy' to show how whisky smugglers made their uisquebaugh. It was a whisky smuggler called James Robertson who turned 'legitimate' and opened the first Lochnagar Distillery in 1826. Queen Victoria liked the Lochnagar whisky. It was delivered to the castle 'in bottles, with an attractive blue and black label, or more generally by the gallon in casks'. If you end your walk with a visit to the distillery you will be able to taste it for yourself.

Whisky bothy at Lochnagar Distillery.

Royal Lochnagar Distillery.

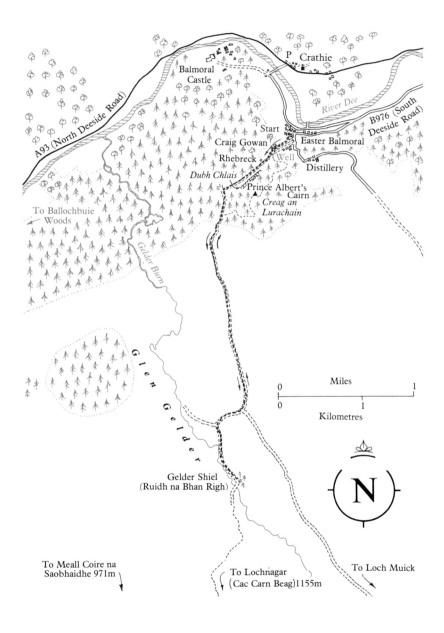

GLEN GELDER

When Empress Eugenie of France visited Queen Victoria at Balmoral in October 1879, she was taken on a trip to Ruidh na Bhan Righ – the Queen's Shiel. 'It stands in a very wild solitary spot looking up to Loch-na-Gar, which towers up immediately above the house', Victoria wrote in her Diary, 'though to reach Loch-na-gar itself would take a very long time'. The solitary spot is in Glen Gelder. This route by the Gelder Burn is a peaceful back door to Lochnagar. Largely left to climbers heading for the corries, it offers a different approach and a dramatically different view of the mountain.

The starting point is Easter Balmoral, where three estate roads meet near the entrance to the castle grounds. Take the one starting at the local grocer's shop. It climbs up past a number of estate houses, with Craig Gowan on the right. Note the granite memorial well at the approach to the house.

Watch out for a narrow path going off uphill on the left near Craig Gowan. This takes you up Creag an Lurachain or Lurgainn, where Queen Victoria built a huge memorial pyramid to Prince Albert. It can be seen for miles around – and anyone who stands at its base feels like a pygmy. It is well worth the diversion. The path to it loops around the hill and back on to the Gelder road.

INFORMATION

Distance return:
9.5 km (6 miles).

Start and finish:
Easter Balmoral. From the A93, cross the bridge at Crathie, turn left at the Balmoral Castle gates, and go along the B976 for 1 km. Turn right up a steep brae towards the Royal Lochnagar Distillery. Halfway up the brae, opposite Strachan's shop, a road goes left to the village hall, cars can be parked there.

Terrain: Good track all the way to Gelder Shiel. Rough track peters out beyond the Shiel and the ground near the loch is wet and boggy. Boots or strong shoes recommended.

Refreshments:
Tearoom at the distillery.

Opening hours
The Tourist Information Centre in the car park at Crathie is open Easter to October. The Royal Lochnagar Distillery has a Visitor Centre, open Easter-Oct, Mon-Sat 10.00–17.00, Sun 11.00–16.00, Nov-Mar Mon-Fri 10.00–17.00.

Gelder Shiel.

From Craig Gowan the main track climbs up to a gate at Rhebreck. Through the gate it continues uphill, with woodland on the right and a high cliff on the left known as Dubh Chlais, the black hollow. When you reach a fork in the road go left. The track dips and rises again until it breaks clear of the woods. Opening up in front of you is a striking panorama of the Gelder valley, with Lochnagar looming up in the distance.

Deer can often be seen on your right, grazing on the banks of the Gelder Burn. On the far side of the burn you will see a long dark line cutting across the face of the moor towards the Ballochbuie woods. This is The Ditch, a trench 1.5m deep and 1.5 km long. Prince Albert had it dug out of the heather so that he could cross the moor out of sight of the deer, popping up now and again to take pot-shots at them. The fastidious Prince didn't like crawling on his stomach in the heather and getting his clothes dirty.

Your track runs parallel with the Gelder for about 2 km before it splits in two. The way ahead leads to Allt-na-giubhsaich and the Spittal of Glenmuick, but you go right to the Gelder Shiel, which nestles in a tiny wood on the east bank of the river. There is another junction a short distance ahead, one route going on to Ballochbuie Forest, which Queen Victoria called 'the bonniest plaid in Scotland'. The other branch turns sharp left to the shiel.

Ruidh na Bhan Righ, the Queen's Shiel (the name is above the door) stands on an idyllic site, a solid granite building, with the Gelder Burn on its doorstep, while farther up the glen the clouds dip and roll over the corries on Lochnagar. Victoria said the Shiel contained 'only two small rooms and a kitchen.' It is an ideal picnic spot. The Queen and Empress Eugenie had tea and trout there, the fish caught by John Brown. To-day, members of the Royal Family probably eat hamburgers when they picnic at the Shiel, for outside the door a wooden structure has been built for holding barbecues.

Royal ponies still clip-clop up the track by the Gelder Burn (tethering posts can be seen at different points), but the stable across the path from Ruidh na Bhan Righ was long ago opened up to climbers and

Lochnagar.

hillwalkers as a howff in which to shelter from the storms of Lochnagar. From here, climbers head for the main corrie, or go straight to the summit by Meall Coire na Saobhaidhe – the hill of the corrie of the foxes' den. Interestingly, there is a Foxes' Well on the route to the Lochnagar summit from Allt-na-guibhsaich.

Although our walk ends at the Shiel, some may want to go beyond it. The track from the Shiel crosses a wooden bridge and pushes towards Lochnagar for a mile. After that it disappears and the going gets wet, rough and rocky. It is not an easy walk, but there is a lot of satisfaction for those who go all the way to the loch which gave Lochnagar its name. The highest point on Lochnagar, Cac Carn Beag, is 1154 m (3786 ft). The loch lies at 785 m (2575 ft) and is 370 m (1200 ft) below the plateau, of which half is cliff. Here, you have a close-up view of the corries that make Lochnagar familiar to hundreds of people travelling up Deeside.

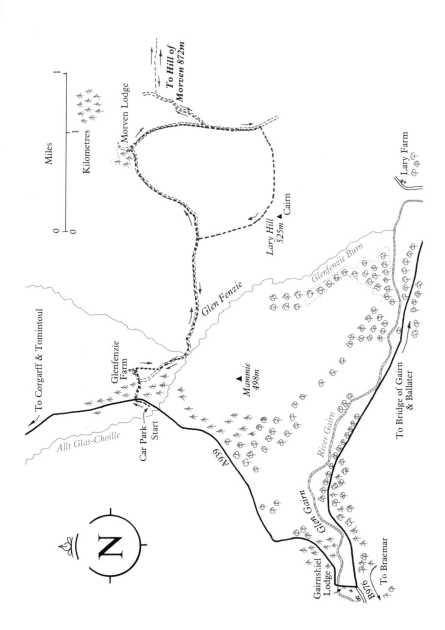

To Hill of Morven 872m

Morven Lodge

Miles

Kilometres

Lary Farm

Lary Hill
525m Cairn

Glen Fenzie

Glenfenzie Burn

To Corgarff & Tomintoul

Glenfenzie Farm

Mammie
498m

To Bridge of Gairn
& Ballater

Car Park
Start

Allt Glas-Choille

A939

River Gairn

Glen Gairn

N

Gairnshiel
Lodge

B976   To Braemar

MORVEN LODGE

A spider's web of tracks converge on Morven – Mor Bheinn, the 'big hill' behind Ballater. One comes up the Deskry Water from Boutie's, the old drovers' inn at Boultenstone, near Tarland, while others push towards it from Logie-Coldstone, Tullich, the Pass of Ballater and Glen Gairn. The most attractive approach to the hill, however, is by a burn that comes tumbling out of the hills near Gairnshiel.

From the layby, walk up the road for about 150m and take a track on the right which goes uphill through a scattering of pine trees – this is the start of the route to Morven. Where it forks, go left around a loop that passes Glenfenzie Farm and rejoins the main track further on.

Glenfenzie is a ruin now, its roof shattered, its windows gaping to the sky, its outbuildings empty and deserted. Inside the house is a large 'swey' fireplace, conjuring up images of broth pots bubbling over a smoky peat fire. A swey was a movable, swinging iron bar from which pots and kettles were hung.

Outside, there are other reminders of the days when people lived here. On one of the granite stones on the front wall of the house are the initials 'DM' and the date 1879, while at the opposite end of the wall, another stone has the date 1822.

INFORMATION

Distance: 6 km (4 miles), add 1.5 km (1 mile) for Lary Hill.

Start and finish: Layby on the A939. From the A93 between Ballater and Braemar, turn onto the A939 Tomintoul road. Cross Gairnshiel Bridge and continue for about 3 km until you reach a green bridge beside a lone pine tree. Park beneath the tree.

Terrain: The main tracks are in good condition, but if you return by Lary Hill the path is rough and indistinct in places. Boots recommended: take waterproofs and OS Landranger map 37.

Refreshments: None en route.

Glenfenzie Farm.

Whoever lived in Glenfenzie Farm last century had a magnificent view from the front window. The farm is perched on the side of a hill. From it you look down the long sweep of the valley, over a great rash of juniper bushes and across distant fields to the dome-like outline of Mount Keen.

As you follow the track downhill, the ruins of other buildings can be seen. The Glenfenzie Burn cuts across the track and turns off through Glen Fenzie on its way to join the River Gairn. The burn has to be crossed by stepping stones, and from there the track goes left, climbing uphill towards a quarry. Lary Hill is on the right, another rough track rising towards the top of it from a point near the quarry. The track you are on continues uphill and then drops down towards the site of Morven Lodge.

The lodge stood in a green basin at the foot of the 'big hill', sheltered by pine trees. The track from Glenfenzie goes through this tiny wood, and deer can sometimes be seen grazing there. The lodge, owned by Alexander Keiller, the Dundee 'jam king' at the end of last century, was an imposing building, bustling with life when the gentry gathered there during the shooting season.

In 1891, Keiller built a second Morven Lodge nearer Ballater and demolished the old one. Today, only traces of the original lodge can be seen, but there are still a number of abandoned buildings scattered about the grassy hollow where it stood – the stables, a laundry, the keeper's house and the shepherd's house. The pillared gateway at the entrance to the drive is a last link with Morven's lost glory. As for the 'new' Morven Lodge, it still draws hundreds of visitors, but they know it not as Morven but as the Craigendarroch Hotel and Country Club.

Morven itself is a great oblong lump of a hill. It is not part of this walk, but if you want to get to the 872m summit it is not too difficult. From the lodge you can see a track running along the side of the hill, and from there it is a comparatively easy climb up grassy slopes to the top. You should, however, be well equipped with waterproofs, boots, map and compass – the weather can change rapidly at any time of the year.

From the old lodge, the return can be made either by going back the way you came, retracing your steps to Glenfenzie Farm, or by going over Lary Hill, from where you will get marvelloous panoramic views. If you plump for the Lary route, leave the lodge by the main drive, through the now redundant gateway, and take the estate road running south to Lary Farm. About 1.5km from the lodge you will come to a fence and gate. Beyond the gate, a rough path goes up Lary Hill on the right. Stick close to the fence and this will take you over the hill and back down to the main track.

Laundry at Morven Lodge.

As you near the top of the hill the path disappears; just head for the highest cairn on the summit. From here you get a grandstand view of the Deeside hills: Morven behind you, Mount Keen in the distance to the south, Cairn Leuchan, the Coyles of Muick, Lochnagar and Ben Avon with its wart-like tors.

Place-name experts have different theories about the origin of the name Lary. Some say it may come from larach, a ruin, which seems improbable; the old Gaelic speakers in Glen Gairn said it came from lairig, a pass. This is more likely – Glen Fenzie, which runs along the foot of Lary Hill, was at one time a route taking travellers up by Laggan and on to Tornahaish and Strathdon.

Facing Lary Hill across the Glenfenzie Burn is another small hill with the curious name of Mammie which, although it has a maternal ring about it, simply means a little round hill.

From your bigger round hill, Lary, make your way down towards the Morven Lodge track. Keep to the right of the cairn and stick closely to the broken fence on your right. Soon you will pick up the track that you first saw when you passed the quarry on the outward route. It is a rough, stony track, though quite wide, and care should be taken going downhill.

From the quarry, make your way back to the road and the parking place, missing out the loop to Glenfenzie Farm.

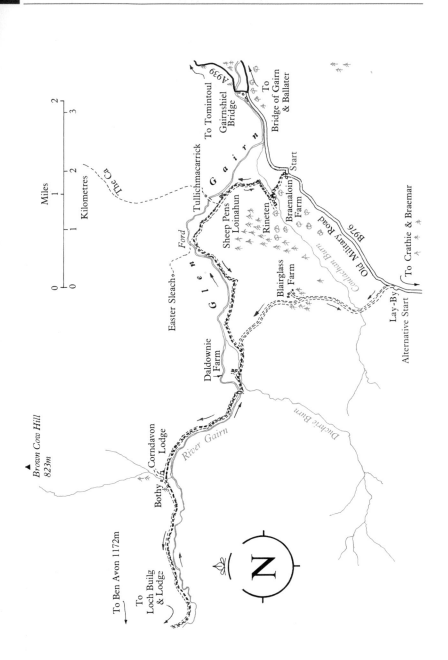

Brown Cow Hill
823m

To Ben Avon 1172m

To
Loch Builg
& Lodge

Bothy

Corndavon
Lodge

River Gairn

Daldownie
Farm

Easter Sleach

Ford

The Ca

Tullichmacarrick

Sheep Pens
Loinahun

Rineten

Blairglass
Farm

Braenaloin
Farm

Start

To Tomintoul

A939

Gairnshiel
Bridge

To
Bridge of Gairn
& Ballater

Coulachan Burn

Old Military Road

B976

To Crathie & Braemar

Lay-By

Alternative Start

Duchrie Burn

Miles
0   1   2

Kilometres
0   1   2   3

N

GLEN GAIRN

The glen of memories – that's Glen Gairn, whose river is the longest tributary of the Dee. From its source high on Ben Avon, the Water of Gairn flows east for over 30 km until it reaches its outlet at a point called the Fit o' Gairn, near Ballater. Amy Stewart Fraser, whose book, *The Hills of Home*, became a best-seller and put Glen Gairn on the map, wrote about how this once well-populated glen had been emptied of its folk, leaving only larachs and deserted 'ferm-touns'.

The 7 km stretch from the Fit o' Gairn to Gairnshiel is still well cultivated, but as you go west life begins to ebb from the glen. It is near Gairnshiel, where a track stretches away to Ben Avon (pronounced Ben A'an), that this walk begins, not far from where the great hump-backed Gairnshiel Bridge loups the Gairn water and carries the old military road north to Corgarff.

There is no easy access to the track from the bridge itself, so it has to be approached from the roadside farm of Braenaloin, 1.5 km south-west of Gairnshiel (10 km from Ballater) on the B976 road to Crathie. Follow the Braenaloin track past the farm and go downhill to Rineten, where the path goes through a gate, turns right and then veers left towards the Gairn. You can join the track by a slightly shorter route branching off the Crathie road (see Information), but the Braenaloin route is recommended.

INFORMATION

Distance return:
14 km (9 miles) from Braenaloin. Add 10 km (6 miles) for Loch Builg.

Start and finish: Braenaloin Farm. From the A93 west of Ballater, turn right onto the A939 Tomintoul road. At Gairnshiel, in 6km, fork left. Braenaloin is 1.5 km further on.

There is an alternative approach to Corndavon from the Gairnshiel-Crathie road. Halfway between Gairnshiel and Crathie, look for a large layby from where a wide, rough track goes down to a gate. This track crosses the Coulachan Burn and passes Blairglass Farm on its way to the River Gairn, where it joins the track from Braenaloin near the ruins of Daldownie.

Terrain: Good track all the way from Braenaloin. Strong shoes or boots advised.

Refreshments: None en route. Nearest in Ballater.

This bridge over the Gairn was originally planned for an extension to the Royal line from Ballater.

The track from Braenaloin is broad and clearly defined, running parallel with the river, and you follow it all the way to Corndavon and Loch Builg. Across the river is the abandoned farm of Tullichmacarrick, and not far away on the right is another ruin, all that is left of the minister's house. From this spot, a century ago, he walked to Sunday services in the kirk at the Bridge of Gairn, summer and winter, in wind, rain and snow.

A family outing in Glen Gairn. In the background are the ruins of Daldownie Farm.

There are sheep pens on the south side of the river, for Glengairn is sheep country. It is deserted now, but nearly a century and a half ago the manse, which was at an altitude of 370 m, looked down on a hamlet of six or eight cottages called Loinahun. One of the residents in Loinahun was an old weaver whose wife was a relative of John Brown, Queen Victoria's famous attendant. The Queen often gave gifts of shawls and tea and tobacco to the old couple as she drove up the glen on one of her expeditons into the hills.

There is a bridge over the Gairn at Tullichmacarrick, and behind it a track climbs up the hill on its way to Corgarff. This is the Ca, the old route from Glengairn to Upper Donside. The name is an old Scots word meaning a way for cattle out to the rough ground', and rough it certainly is, for the path itself has almost disappeared in places.

As you make your way along the glen yet another roofless farmhouse, Easter Sleach, comes into view across the river. It must have been a lonely place, high up on the hill, reached by a farm track from a ford across the Gairn. All along this stretch of the glen there are ruins marking the sites of former crofts and cottar houses, but you have to look for them. Ian Murray, in his book *In the Shadow of Lochnagar*, said he counted 75 recognisable dwellings in the glen.

The river, twisting and turning as it tumbles down from its head stream on Ben Avon, marks your route through the glen. About 3 km from Braenaloin, the track begins to climb and the river loops away from it. Soon you will find yourself looking down on a grassy hollow where sheep graze near the ruins of Daldownie Farm.

Until it was demolished in 1977 Daldownie was the last farmhouse of any consequence in the glen. The folk there came to their door to wave to Queen Victoria as she rode past on her way into the hills, but all that is left of it now is a red-roofed barn and a rickle of stones – and maybe the fairies. The Daldownie farmer swore that there were fairies there. He heard their revels during the night and saw their footprints outside his house in the morning. There is a spot behind the house known as An Sidhean, the fairy hill.

Before the track drops down to Daldownie it meets up with another track coming in on the left – the alternative route from the Crathie road. Near the ruins it is carried over the Duchrie Burn by a small wooden bridge, while a little farther on there is a full-size iron bridge that, if things had been different, might have carried railway traffic from Ballater to Braemar. This bridge was built when an extension to the Deeside line was planned, and it should have crossed the river at the Fit of Gairn. However, Queen Victoria didn't like the idea of locomotive engines puffing past her castle with trainloads of tourists and put a stop to it, so the railway bridge became a road bridge and was moved to its present site near Daldownie.

Upstream, not far from the bridge, are the remains of another failed project – what appears to have been a double dyke on the opposite side of the river. It is, in fact, a small channel that was to be part of a mill

planned for this corner of Gairnside, but, like the Pit o'
Gairn bridge, nothing came of it.

Once over the Gairn bridge you are heading for lumpy
Ben Avon. The road winds gently through scenery
that becomes softer and gentler. But there is yet
another ruin to see, although this one wasn't the result
of depopulation and demolition. Corndavon Lodge, a
shooting lodge for Royalty on the banks of the Gairn,
was almost completely destroyed by fire. Only one
corner of it remains intact. It still carries a faint air of
forgotten grandeur. Trees, rising on the high ground
behind the lodge, sheltered it from the north. Lord
Cardigan, of Crimean fame, was its tenant for a
number of years, while in more recent times King
George VI shot over the Corndavon moors.

Ruins of Corndavon Lodge.

Corndavon must have been an impressive Royal
'howff' in its time, like so many other solid granite
shooting lodges built in 'the back of beyond'. Some of
the beds were hung with tartan which was said to have
been at Culloden. In the large room which survived
the fire, the walls have been decorated with a huge
mural showing deer grazing in the hills around the
Lodge. If you are tall enough you may be able to peep
through the windows and see it.

The hill country around Corndavon is not as
romantic-looking as the mural on the lodge, but it has
certain quiet charm. Beyond the Lodge and separated
by a small burn is an out-building which once housed
the staff and has now been turned into a bothy for hill-
walkers. The work was done by the Grampian

Transport Hillwalking Club, and if there is such a thing as a Best Bothy Award, Corndavon would win it hands down. It has been turned into a shelter fit for kings; upstairs there is even a lounge complete with sofa. George VI would certainly have given it a Royal thumbs up.

Bothy at Corndavon.

Not far from the lodge is a hill marked on the OS map as Brown Cow Hill. In local dialect it is known as the Broon Coo. It is supposed to look like a brown cow, but it was once said that it looked more like a whale. When snow lies late in its corrie it is known as the Broon Coo's White Calf.

The hills close in as you push up the glen and come to the last house on the walk – Lochbuilg Lodge. Not surprisingly, this is also a ruin. Donald McHardy, a stalker, lived here with his wife and family. The lodge stood on a knoll overlooking Lochan Feurach and Lochan Orr, two of a group of tiny lochans just before you reach Loch Builg. The loch marks the meeting place of a trio of vital routes through the hills; one through Gairnside (the route you have taken), a second by the Bealach Dearg, the Red Pass, to Invercauld and Braemar, and a third along a path by Loch Builg to Inchrory and Tomintoul.

Loch Builg is a cold and desolate spot. There is a rickety boathouse on the edge of the loch, sometimes used by hill-walkers and climbers going up Ben Avon, whose knotted brow looks down on this cross-roads in the hills. Someone once chalked across the wall, 'Welcome to the highest boathouse in the country. Peace and love to you all'. It was a nice friendly message to greet you at the end of a long trek.

Here, on the shores of Loch Builg, we turn on our tracks and go back the way we came – back through the glen of memories.

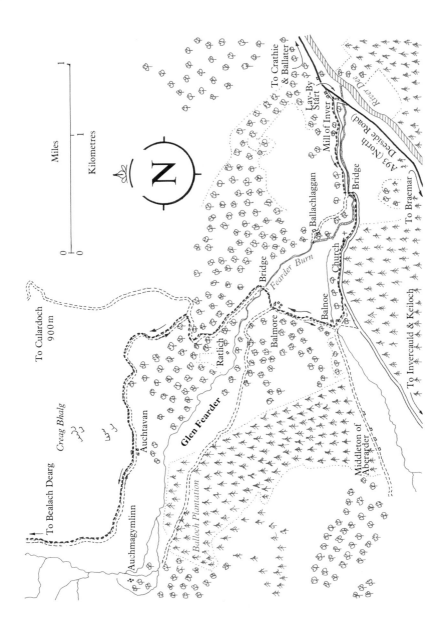

GLEN FEARDER

The grave of a giant – the last of his race – can be found in remote Glen Fearder on upper Deeside. At least that is what some people believe, and if you want to go giant-hunting, the place to start is at the Mill of Inver. Look for a signpost saying 'Aberarder'.

On the other side of the A93, at the mouth of the Fearder Burn, a narrow road goes up to Ballachlaggan, where 18 troublesome 'bonnet lairds' (tenant farmers) were once hung in the 'gryt barn at Aberardir' by order of the laird of Invercauld. Near a wooden bridge over the Fearder Burn a farm track leaves the road, crosses a cattle grid, and goes straight ahead to Ballachlaggan, but your route is over the bridge, following the line of the burn.

In about 1.5 km from the main road you reach the old mission church of Aberarder, which became a school, then a storehouse for farm fodder. It now stands empty and neglected, its kirk bell hanging silently from the belfry.

The road meanders on through woodland to a junction where the main track goes left to Keiloch, at the entrance to Invercauld Estate, while you follow the right-hand branch down towards the farm at Balnoe. The road splits again, one route turning left towards Middleton of Aberarder, where ruined cottages tell of more depopulation, and the other going on past Balnoe to the deserted farm of Balmore.

Your route is by Balmore, passing through a gate before reaching the abandoned farm. Beyond the farmhouse the road turns left and heads for the forestry plantation at Balloch, but the route to Glen Fearder lies straight ahead, through a field with a red metal gate. The track runs down the edge of the field and leaves it by another gate. Make sure that you close all gates behind you (unless you found them open).

The road running from Aberarder past Balnoe is the old drove road through the Gairn hills to the north. It went over the east shoulder of Culardoch to Loch Builg and from there on to Tomintoul. It became a

INFORMATION

Distance return: 9.5 km (6 miles). Add 1.5 km (1 mile) for Auchnagymlinn.

Start and finish: Mill of Inver layby on A93, 14 km west of Ballater. About 3km after passing Crathie, look for a small cottage (an old tollhouse) on the right. The layby is just beyond it on the left.

Terrain: Good road to Balnoe, but across the bridge at Balmore it is a rough track. Nearer to Auchtavan the track is rough and often wet. Boots or strong shoes recommended.

Refreshments: None en route. Toilets and a seasonal tourist information centre at Crathie.

public road at the end of last century, but was eventually ousted by other routes.

Beyond the second gate at Balmore, the track crosses the Fearder Burn by a wooden bridge, meets up with a path from Ballachlaggan and swings left, climbing through thick woodland. There is another gate well up the hill. Look down through the trees on your left and you will see a ruined building not far from the Fearder Burn. This is all that remains of St Manire Chapel, near the farm of Ratlich. At one time a market was held there, but it moved to Clachanturn, near Crathie.

The track swings right and pushes uphill until it reaches a junction. The right branch is the old route to Culardoch, but your route is to the left, through a stretch of moorland where an amazing regeneration of birch trees has taken place. Here too, orchids and other wild flowers can be seen. The track gets rough, wet and muddy in places, so mind your step.

From this track you get a breathtaking 'back door' view of Lochnagar. It is different from any other view you may have seen of Deeside's famous mountain and when the clouds are chasing each other in and out of the gullies it does take your breath away. The Queen Mother often saw it this way.

Auchtavan, Royal shiel nestling in the Deeside hills.

When you come to a dyke that marks the start of the Auchtavan lands you will discover her hideaway. Near the dyke, a number of ruined cottages point to the existence of a fair-sized community at one time. Note the kiln on the right-hand side of the track. As you go downhill, with the Fearder glen opening out ahead, you will see a tidy little cottage nestling in the lap of Creag Bhalg - the Queen Mother's Shiel.

The Shiel is kept in good condition, though it is rarely used now. Nearby are the roofless shells of old 'black houses'. One building on the right did have a roof. It was made of corrugated iron, but when this was blown off a second roof was exposed – an old 'thacket' roof.

Take a look at the chimneypot, which has also suffered from the Fearder gales. It is made of wood, as is the 'hingin' lum' inside the house. It sounds like a dangerous fire hazard, but the use of peat in the days of 'hinging' lums' made it reasonably safe.

The track goes past the back of the Queen Mother's Shiel and a short distance beyond it, comes to a high deer fence with a gate. From there it continues along the side of Creag Bhalg until it turns right at the head of Glen Fearder and wanders through the grey moors towards the old Bealach Dearg, the red pass, with another path cutting off to Culardoch.

Old cottage at Auchtavan, with thatched roof beneath a corrugated iron one.

Where the track turns north beyond Auchtavan, look down into the head of the glen and you will see a ruined settlement near the Fearder Burn. This is, or was, Auchnagymlinn, once the highest farm in the glen. Today the highest farm is Auchtavan, a name which in Gaelic means 'the field of the two kids', an indication that the rent paid to the laird of Invercauld was two young goats.

Fearder, on the other hand, means 'the glen of the high water' or perhaps 'the bog of high water', which says something about the conditions people there had to contend with in bygone days. It must have taken giants of men to carve a living out of this dour corner of the north-east. In fact, old tales suggest that they were giants.

The Deeside historian and writer A. I. McConnochie said you could see the grave of a giant at Auchnagymlinn – and that the grave was six metres long! There is another story, probably nearer to the truth. It says that members of a family which once lived in the forks of the Fearder Burn were all over seven feet (2.2m) tall, and that they all died young. It is unlikely that you will find any trace of giants now, for in the Muckle Spate of 1829, Auchnagymlinn was destroyed by sand and gravel.

Those with a liking for a long tramp can follow the Auchtavan track to the Bealach Dearg (crossing two burns on the way) and return through Invercauld to Keiloch and the A93, but car arrangements would have to be made. The easier way is to return the way you came, down to the old drove road and on by Balmore to Balnoe and Inver.

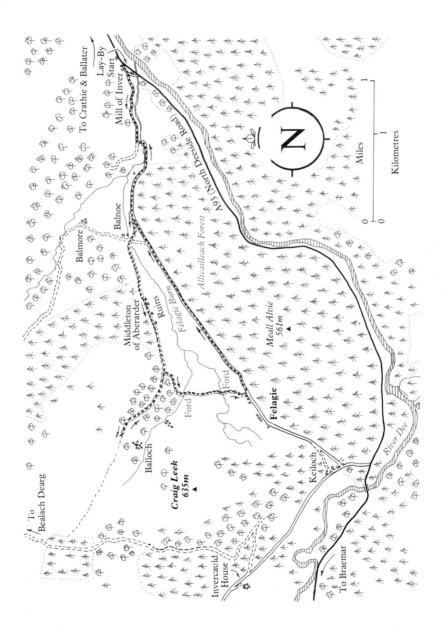

FELAGIE AND CRAIG LEEK

The Felagie Burn takes its name from the Gaelic feith leaghaidh, the slow burn. It wanders lazily through the district of Aberarder on the Invercauld Estate, near Braemar, which lies on the approaches to the Bealach Dearg, the red pass, once the main droving route to the south. It was a well-populated corner of Upper Deeside at one time.

The first part of the walk, past the old mission church of Aberarder towards Balnoe, is the same as in walk 18. At the fork before Balnoe, turn left by a bridge crossing the Felagie Burn.

Here you follow an old track that runs by Middleton of Aberarder along the north side of the glen towards the 635m Craig Leek, a rocky hill east of the Bealach Dearg. The Aberarder track echoes with memories of the past, for at almost every step, crumbling ruins remind you of the time when people lived and worked in this quiet glen. The remains of their homes can be seen on both sides of the track, some in the fenced-off woodland on the right.

They are empty shells now, but in 1810 the school at Aberarder had no fewer than 120 pupils on the roll – 80 boys and 40 girls. By 1821 the number had dropped to 62, and when it closed a century later, there were only two pupils. In his book *The Old Deeside Road*, G. M. Fraser recalled that in 1921 you could 'find there scarcely a soul except at the few huts at Middleton'.

The first ruined house on the Middleton of Aberarder road was the old school before it moved to the mission church. Near this ruin an unlocked gate crosses the track. Here, a large area of moorland has been fenced off to keep out the deer, enclosing the old clachan, and further up the track is another gate, this one locked, but the old road has not been completely shut off.

Before you reach the second gate, keep an eye open for a small gate a little way up the hill at the end of the wood. This gate takes you onto a narrow footpath which runs parallel with the fence and turns down onto the Aberarder track. Make sure that you secure the gate firmly behind you.

INFORMATION

Distance return:
8 km (5 miles). Add about 3 km (2 miles) for the Upper Balloch settlement.

Start and finish:
Layby at Inver on A93. See walk 18 for details.

Terrain: Flat and easy, apart from Craig Leek, but boots or strong shoes are recommended. Take waterproofs.

Refreshments: None en route.

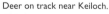
Deer on track near Keiloch.

After this detour, follow the track towards Craig Leek until you come to a stream running down to join the Felagie Burn. A ford is marked on the map here. Local people used it when they crossed the moor to the south side of the glen, and this is your route back to Inver, but for the moment stick to the Middleton of Aberarder track as it bears right, uphill.

The track, which takes you to the ruins of two old settlements, is a continuation of a route, starting at Inver, which runs through the clachan of Middleton of Aberarder and climbs through a pass shown on old maps as Am Bealach (which simply means 'the pass'), eventually linking up with the Bealach Dearg. The Craig Leek track fades out as you climb, but when you come to a heap of stones on higher ground, bear left over a grassy area towards a line of trees on the ridge ahead.

The stones came from the 'steening' (stone clearing) of the land by the crofters, and piles of them can be seen scattered on various parts of the hill. This grassy hollow was at one time well cultivated, as the maps show, and the ruins of old holdings run hard into the gut of Am Bealach, sprawling uphill towards the road to the Bealach Dearg.

The two settlements were known as Upper and Lower Balloch, from bealach, a pass or hill-crossing, and in the higher settlement the clear line of a street can be picked out, with houses on either side. Some of the ruins lie on the opposite side of the burn which runs downhill through the settlements to the Felagie Burn.

From this high and windy spot you have an eagle's eye view of the Felagie glen. Craig Leek is said to be one of the finest viewpoints in the district, and it is easy to see why. From the track or from Craig Leek itself you look back on a breathtaking view of Lochnagar and the Stuic.

Up above the Balloch settlements a track curves away towards the Bealach Dearg. That way lies an alternative route to Keiloch and back to Inver, but it is not part of the present walk.

The return route is back the way you came, leaving the glories of Craig Leek and making your way down towards Aberarder and the Felagie Burn. Near the ford, keep an eye open for a tall flagpole – it marks the site of an old shooting range used in the time of the Boer War. Pieces of the targets can still be found scattered in the heather.

Ford the burn (a few easy steps) and make your way across the moor on a track crossing the Felagie Burn and linking up with the road from Inver. In winter the path over the moor can be wet and marshy – the burn is known as 'the bog-stream'. Once on the road, turn left for Inver. To the right lies Keiloch at the entrance to the Invercauld estate. There is an East Grampian Deer Management Group notice at Keiloch welcoming hillwalkers and visitors but asking them not to disturb the deer during the shooting season.

Deer feeding in Aberarder.

The road, which runs almost parallel to the A93, passes under the foot of Meall Alvie (560m) and follows the line of Alltcailleach Forest. Some people say this was once part of the Old Deeside Road, and that it was also one of General Wade's military roads, but this has never been proved.

At any rate, it was a busy road, even being used as an alternative to the main Deeside road in the early days of motoring. Before that, in the latter part of the 19th century, it was repaired and linked up with the north route to the River Gairn by Balnoe and Balmore. The idea was to provide an alternative to the Bealach Dearg, avoiding the deer forests there.

Hill-walker feeding deer on Invercauld estate.

There was also a Felagie village on this 'new' road, a group of about ten houses east of Keiloch. The village and its name can still be seen on some maps, and the ruins are there as a reminder of the 'lost' community. But all that is in the past. Middleton of Aberarder, the Craig Leek holdings and Felagie village have all gone. This long, wide glen and its lazy burn are left to the sheep and the deer. In winter, great herds of deer come down to the Felagie glen to be fed by the Invercauld keepers.

The walk along the south side of the glen is an easy one, taking you back to the old church at Aberarder and then down to your car at Inver.

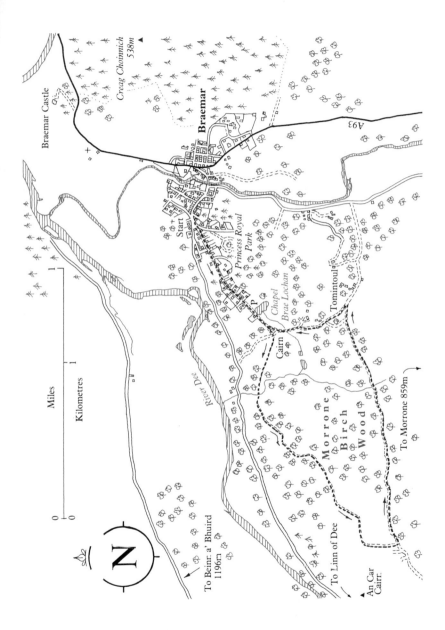

Braemar Castle

Creag Choinnich 538m

Braemar

A93

Start

Princess Royal Park

P

Chapel Brae Lochan

Cairn

Tomintoul

Morrone Birch Wood

To Morrone 859m

An Car Cairn.

To Linn of Dee

River Dee

To Beinn a' Bhuird 1196m

Miles

Kilometres

N

MORRONE BIRCH WOOD

One of the best examples of an upland birch wood in Britain can be seen on the lower slopes of Morrone, the 859m hill dominating Braemar. Its name, by the way, is another variation of Morven, meaning simply 'big hill'. There is a weather recording station on the summit. The Morrone birch wood is designated as a National Nature Reserve by Scottish Natural Heritage.

This walk takes a pleasant circular route through the lower part of the wood and across moorland where there are good views down to the Dee Valley. From the west end of the village, near the Princess Royal park, where the famous Braemar Gathering is held each year on the first Saturday in September, walk up Chapel Brae to a small lochan on the left. There is a rough car park here. The lochan, known locally as the duckpond, is the haunt of mallard ducks - wild birds, but tamed by tourism, for whenever a car appears they come waddling over looking for titbits.

On the track that passes the pond there is a sign saying 'Morrone Birch Wood'. Follow the track until you come to a nature reserve cairn, where the track forks, one branch going downhill towards the Linn of Dee road, the other running along the side of a fence into the wood.

Take the path by the fence. As it meanders through the wood, it gives you glimpses of the road below and the hills across the Dee. In early summer, alpine plants carpet the ground and later the heather turns to

INFORMATION

Distance: 5 km (3 miles).

Start and finish: Princess Royal park, Braemar.

Terrain: Woodland tracks and paths through heather. Can be muddy underfoot in wet weather. Strong shoes or wellies recommended.

Refreshments: Wide choice in Braemar.

Opening hours Braemar Heritage Centre, The Mews. Open daily all year, but reduced hours in winter. Information and displays on the Cairngorms and the Braemar area as well as general tourist information. Braemar Castle, 1 km north-east of the village, is well worth a visit, though it is not on this walk. Open May–early Oct daily 10.00–18.00.

The 'duck pond' at Morrone birch wood.

purple, splashing Morrone with colour. But it is the 'dainty lady' of the forest, the silver birch, that holds sway. The birch is small, sometimes no more than 5m in height, and seldom more than 10m. The Morrone birch wood extends up to over 600m on the northern slopes of the hill, and at its upper edge it is close to the maximum altitude for tree growth.

Juniper bushes proliferate beside and beneath the birch, creeping across the hill as if intent on taking it over. There is a dense growth beneath much of the wood and heavy thickets where the trees thin out. The path pushes on, with stepping-stones taking you over one of the burns that gurgle down from the springs on the hill. In spate, the burns can be tricky to cross and the going on the path itself can be wet after rain. After more stepping-stones, the path begins a gentle climb, passing a waymarker post on the left.

Flooded burn in Morrone birch wood.

Looking back, you can see the Dee looping around Braemar, while ahead is a glimpse of the Quoich glen. Then the path narrows and draws away to the left and onto open moorland, heading towards a distant fence. In the distance you will see a cairn sticking up above the trees beyond the fence. This is An Car, or the Car Prop as it is known locally (a prop is a prominent landmark), and it was at one time popular with visitors, but now it is practically swallowed up by the trees.

Near the fence is a stile which takes you into the forest, but the birch wood track does a U-turn and heads back to Braemar, passing another nature reserve cairn with a map of the area. Away in the distance you can see the great mass of Beinn a'Bhuird, the 'table mountain'. On the return walk the track is wider and higher, well up the slopes of Morrone.

Keep an eye open for roe deer, or even red deer. Notices on enclosures bordering the track tell you that they were fenced off in 1978 to protect the trees from the browsing of deer. The plan was to remove the fences at a later stage and repeat the operation at other points to encourage regeneration.

From the upper track you can see across the great sprawl of moorland and over the birches to the

Deer feeding in Morrone birch wood.

rooftops of Braemar. Facing you to the east is Creag Choinnich - Kenneth's Crag – the hill on the outskirts of Braemar, named after King Kenneth II. Its 538m summit is a splendid viewpoint.

Another track comes up on the left. It will take you back to the car park, but pass it and make for a knoll a short distance ahead, where there is an indicator and a seat. This part of Morrone is known as Tomintoul. The Banffshire Tomintoul claims to be the highest village in the Highlands but, not to be outdone, the Braemar Tomintoul once claimed to have the highest arable land in the country.

The Gaelic origin of Tomintoul is Tom an t-Sabhail, the hill of the barn. The name was given to the highest of a group of crofts on Morrone, and it came to be used collectively for the whole group. It is a superb viewpoint - a good place to survey the surrounding countryside, including the big hills of the Cairngorms, before ending the walk. The various hills can be picked out on an indicator erected by the Deeside Field Club in 1960 to commemorate their 40th anniversary. On the top are four lines of verse written by a former Lord Provost of Aberdeen, the late George Stephen.

Another track goes downhill from the indicator, passing the farmhouse of Tomintoul and leading you back to the lochan, where the ever-hungry ducks will be waiting to greet you. From here it is a short stroll down Chapel Brae back into the village centre.

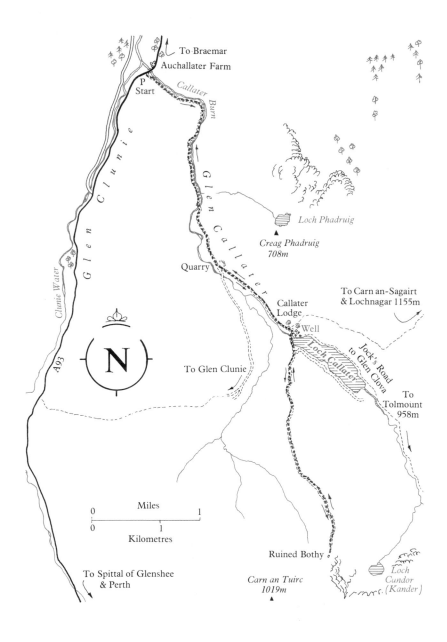

To Braemar
Auchallater Farm

P
Start

Callater Burn

G l e n   C l u n i e

G l e n   C a l l a t e r

Clunie Water

A93

Loch Phadruig

Creag Phadruig
708m

Quarry

To Carn an-Sagairt
& Lochnagar 1155m

Callater
Lodge

Well

Loch Callater

*Jock's Road
to Glen Clova*

N

To Glen Clunie

To
Tolmount
958m

Miles

0 ————————— 1

0 ————————— 1

Kilometres

Ruined Bothy

*Loch
Cundor
(Kander)*

To Spittal of Glenshee
& Perth

*Carn an Tuirc
1019m*
▲

LOCH CALLATER

Loch Callater was once described in an official Deeside survey as an 'idyllic' place. It was not an overstatement, for this is one of the loveliest lochs in the area. From it, paths stretch away to Carn an t-Sagairt and Lochnagar, up by the windy wastes of the Tolmount to Jock's Road and Glen Clova, and onto a high plateau where Prince Albert put a message in a bottle and stuck it in the ground for future generations to discover.

From the car park at Auchallater, a Scottish Rights of Way Society sign points the way, and up a short, stony brae a gate with access for walkers opens up your route through Glen Callater, following the course of the Callater Burn. Here, Nature has sculpted the river rock into weirdly impressive shapes, jagged splinters of stone contrasting sharply with long, flat table-tops beaten smooth by the endless motion of the burn.

The rocks are mostly of micra-slate and granite. Micra-slate was at one time quarried at the lower end of the glen for roofing. The whiter-than-white stones you see in ditches just off the track are limestone, which is more prevalent at the north-west end of Loch Callater.

The glen is hemmed in by high hills. Halfway up there is supposed to be a green hillock inhabited by the 'little folk'. Professor William MacGillivray, a noted 19th century Aberdeen naturalist who roamed these hills and glens, reported in 1850 that a man still living had seen fairies dancing on the hillock, with a piper playing to them.

Myth and magic breed easily in these lonely straths. Callater should really be Patrick or Peter's Glen, for a number of landmarks in and around the glen are called after a priest of that name. About halfway along the glen, where a wooden bridge crosses a burn coming down from the hills on the east, a barely visible path runs alongside it up towards Loch Phadruig.

This tiny loch, hiding behind Craig Phadruig, can't be seen from the glen, but both loch and crag are named after Peter the Priest. Carn an t-Sagairt, which is reached by a path from Loch Callater, is 'the priest's

INFORMATION

Distance return: 10 km (6 miles). Add 6 km (3.5 miles) for Loch Kander.

Start and finish: Auchallater, on A93 3km south of Braemar.

Terrain: Good track all the way to Loch Callater, but path up to Loch Kander is rough and stony. Boots recommended. Take waterproofs and OS Landranger sheet 43.

Refreshments: None en route. Wide selection in Braemar.

Loch Callater.

hill'. All this stems from a miracle performed by Peter when the Braemar area was in the grip of a severe frost that lasted into May.

When a holy well at Loch Callater froze over, leaving the people without water, they called in Peter the Priest. He prayed, the ice melted, and water trickled from the well. Then, as he prayed on, clouds gathered over Carn an t-Sagairt, the frost loosened its grip on the land, and a thaw set in.

The track through this 'miracle' glen is uninterrupted until you come to a quarry on the left. Here the track forks, the right-hand branch going off to Glen Clunie, and the left, which you stay on, to Loch Callater. Soon you will see birch trees rising above an old gamekeeper's lodge near the lochside. The track runs past a gate leading to the front of the lodge, while another track goes behind the house.

Callater Lodge.

Callater Lodge looks out over the loch, which runs south to where deer come down from the high tops to graze on grassy haughs below the Tolmount. The loch, which lies at an altitude of 500m, is about 1.5 km long and covers an area of about 30 hectares. Gulls squawk and dive over its surface and if you are lucky you might see a skein of geese flying low over the water.

Sitting on the grass outside the lodge on a sunny day, looking away to the distant hills, the Deeside survey's description of the scene as 'idyllic' seems to sum it all up. However, the lodge is boarded up and stripped of its porch, a rather sad sight.

But life is coming back to the old stables nearby. In 1993 volunteers from the Mountain Bothies Association restored the building for use as a bothy. Now it provides simple shelter for walkers heading over the Tolmount to Glen Clova, or coming the other way. The path to Clova goes along the east side of the loch, passing a large stone which marks the site of Peter's Well, the scene of Callater's miracle.

From the lodge, looking across a wooden bridge that spans the Callater Burn, a steep, stony track can be seen zigzagging up the steep hill that flanks the loch on the west. This track goes up towards Carn an Tuirc (hill of the boar) and on to a plateau from which you can look down on a remote mountain loch described by one writer as 'lonely, lonely dark Loch Kander'.

The track is easy to follow for most of the way, but it peters out on the plateau. The ground drops away steeply on the left and as you head towards the corrie above Loch Kander, look for what appears to be a pile of stones some way ahead. This is all that remains of an old shepherd's bothy that once looked down on Kander, a rough but-and-ben perched high over what William MacGillivray called 'a recess in the bosom of a mountain'.

Dark Loch Candor.

(Kander)

It is a fairly steep climb and should only be attempted in good conditions by fit walkers, but for those who make the climb, the rewards are great. The views are breathtaking, but even more fascinating is the glimpse you get of Loch Kander, an inky pool far below you. William MacGillivray estimated that the depth of the corrie was about 245m.

He noted that there was a place in the bothy for a small fire, two stone benches, and two recesses in a wall for pipes and other articles. The bothy is now a roofless ruin, but one of the benches can still be seen – and there is still a hole in the wall for the shepherd's pipe.

It can be cold in these high places. When Queen Victoria was there, taking a look at Loch Kander and describing it as 'very wild and dark', she found ice thicker than a shilling coin. It was somewhere near Carn an Tuirc that Prince Albert wrote a message on a bit of paper, put it in a water-bottle, and stuck it in the ground.

You can also make a low-level approach to Loch Kander by walking along the west side of Loch Callater, but the track gives way to a narrow footpath at the end of the loch and finally disappears. Moreover, as you near the opening to Loch Kander the ground becomes wet and boggy.

Whether you make Loch Callater your turning-point, or climb the zigzag track to peer down at Loch Kander, it's a fair bet that you will want to return to this lovely area, for Callater is being 'discovered' by an increasing number of discerning walkers.

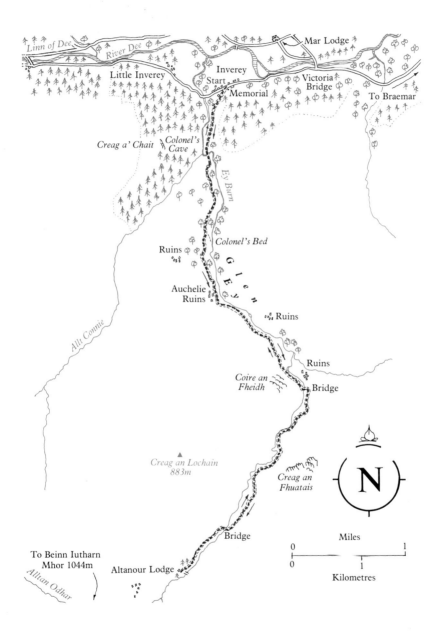

Linn of Dee

River Dee

Mar Lodge

Little Inverey

Inverey

Start

Victoria
Bridge

Memorial

To Braemar

Creag a' Chait

Colonel's
Cave

Ey Burn

Colonel's Bed

Ruins

G l e n   E y

Auchelie
Ruins

Ruins

Allt Connie

Ruins

Coire an
Fheidh

Bridge

Creag an Lochain
883m

Creag an
Fhuatais

N

Bridge

To Beinn Iutharn
Mhor 1044m

Altanour Lodge

Alltan Odhar

Miles		
0		1
0	1	
	Kilometres	

GLEN EY

The mountains of hell – that was what Deeside folk called the two peaks, Beinn Iutharn Mor (1044m) and Beinn Iutharn Bheag (951m) at the head of Glen Ey. In between them is the source of the Ey Burn, which runs down the glen for 12km until it reaches Inverey and the River Dee.

Inverey was where a legendary character called Maggie Gruer lived. In her home at Thistle Cottage, she gave shelter to hundreds of walkers and climbers in the 1930s. She was known to all manner of folk, poets, playwrights and politicians among them, and her homemade oatcakes and thick scones were talked about wherever outdoor folk met. Maggie charged a shilling (5p) for bed and breakfast, or sixpence (2½p) if you were hard up, and she kept the money in a bucket.

The track into the glen starts almost opposite Maggie's house, near a memorial to John Lamont, a native of Inverey, who became the Astronomer Royal of Bavaria. It goes up past a modern house, through a gate, and after crossing a wooden bridge over the Ey Burn, climbs towards a hill on the right.

There was a wood on the hill at one time, but it has virtually disappeared, leaving only a handful of shattered trunks and stumps. Why it died is a mystery, but it may simply have been devastated by the fierce winters in the glen. The same sort of devastation can be seen at Altanour, 8 km up the glen, which is the turning-point of the walk.

This bare, scabbed hill adds a sense of desolation to a glen that still carries the scars of the Clearances, when crofting families were evicted to make way for deer. Five families were moved out in 1829 and resettled elsewhere on the estate. Another eight families were evicted in 1842, along with 3,000 sheep and cattle. A clampdown on illicit whisky distilling speeded up the depopulation, for without this extra income the crofters were unable to pay their rents.

Professor William MacGillivray, in his *Natural History of Deeside and Braemar*, published in 1855, describes

INFORMATION

Distance return: 16 km (10 miles).

Start and finish: Inverey, 6 km west of Braemar on the Linn of Dee road. Please park tidily at the roadside.

Terrain: Good track all the way to Altanour. Boots or strong shoes recommended. Take waterproofs.

Refreshments: None. Nearest in Braemar.

Note: Care is needed if you visit the Colonel's Bed. It is not suitable for young children.

Inverey.

middle Glen Ey as 'a fair green strath, smooth as a well-kept lawn', but he added that there was not a single sheep to be seen. He thought the glen as beautiful as an English park, and in many ways it still is, but the crumbling ruins of deserted settlements give it an air of sadness.

The Colonel's Bed.

About 2 km from Inverey, a small wooden sign at the left edge of the track points to a path that will take you to the Colonel's Bed. It was here, in a narrow ravine on the Ey Burn, that John Farquharson of Inverey, a freebooter better known as the Black Colonel, hid from government troops in 1715.

The path is narrow and in wet weather can be muddy. Where it drops down to the mouth of the Colonel's hiding-place it is often slippery and dangerous. It is inadvisable to take children down here. The 'bed' is a long ledge of slaty rock. It is an awesome place, yet it has its own beauty. Its high, perpendicular cliffs are covered with ferns and flowering plants.

Beyond the Colonel's Bed, the glen becomes green and fertile, with dyked fields spreading out on either side of the track. Now you are in MacGillivray's 'fair green strath', perhaps the loveliest part of the glen, but here too are the reminders of the years of eviction. Up on the right you will see the larachs, the crumbling ruins of old settlements.

Two large ruins can be seen above the track at Auchelie, looking down over the Ey Burn. Two tall larch trees stand outside the houses, untouched by the storms that have stripped so many other trees in the glen. Climb up the hill behind them and you will get a striking view of the Ey Burn as it curves away to the hills at Altanour. The name Auchelie comes from Ach a'Cheiridh, which means 'the field of duskiness'.

The main settlements lay on the opposite side of the river between Auchelie and Creag an Fhuathais, a high, pyramid-shaped hill where the river turns south-west to Altanour. Creag an Fhuathais means 'the crag of the spectre', and there is an old tale that a malicious ghost rolled down huge stones on passers-by, and that something seemed to move along the hillside – 'loathsome, black, shapeless, monstrous' in one account.

Near the foot of Creag an Fhuathais, a wooden bridge which spans the Ey Burn leads to the ruined settlements, which can be seen spreading out on the left. It was among these pathetic ruins that many families lived out their lives in peace until the evictions came. The townships contain the remains of a number of corn-drying kilns, and there are longhouses divided into two or three rooms. In one empty shell you can see flagstones on the ground.

To continue the walk go back to the bridge, where the main track now goes up the east side of the Ey Burn. The river, wriggling and curling through the moorland like a silver serpent, is on your right, and across the water is Corrie an Fheidh – the corrie of the deer. It is well named, for you can often see herds of deer grazing here.

The hills close in as you walk towards Altanour, the Ben Uarns, as they are sometimes called, forming a crescent at the head of the glen. Eventually another bridge takes you back to the west side of the river for the final stretch up to Altanour.

Ruined cottage in Glen Ey, with Creag an Fhuathais in background.

The old shooting lodge takes its name from Alltan Odhar (the dun burn), a tributary of the Ey Burn. The lodge is a sad night now, so ruinous that there is little left. It was still standing at the turn of the century, but was seldom used. The wood which sheltered it has met the same fate, withering away as if stricken by some terrible disease. Dead trees lie all around, and many people find this an eerie spot.

Beyond Altanour are more ruins, all that is left of the summer sheilings used by the crofters. Deeper still into the glen are the mountains of hell, where you may see eagles quartering the sky. Your way, however, is back down the glen, past the corrie of the deer and under the brooding brow of Creag an Fhuathais, where people once fled from a ghost which 'made their hair stand on end and their flesh creep with inexpressible horror'.

Despite the ghost, the ruins and the dying trees, Glen Ey is a delightful place in which to walk. Your only regret at the end of the day will be that there is no Maggie Gruer waiting at Inverey to pour you a cup of tea from her ever-ready teapot and to offer you thick scones and home-made oatcakes.

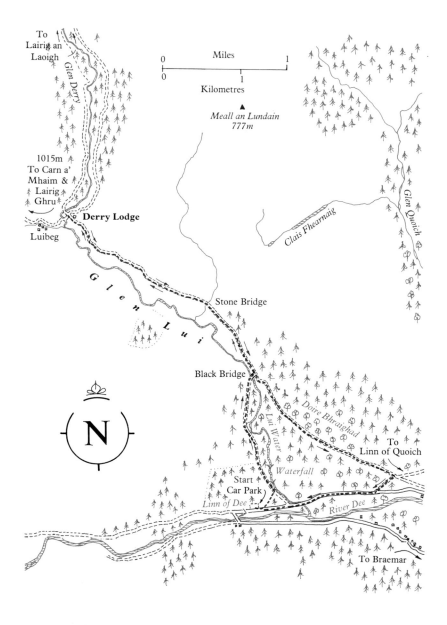

To
Lairig an
Laoigh

Glen Derry

Miles
0 _____ 1

Kilometres
0 _____ 1

Meall an Lundain
777m

1015m
To Carn a'
Mhaim &
Lairig
Ghru

Derry Lodge

Luibeg

Clais Fhearnaig

Glen Quoich

G l e n   L u i

Stone Bridge

Black Bridge

Doire Bhraighad

Lui Water

To
Linn of Quoich

N

Waterfall

Start
Car Park

Linn of Dee

River Dee

To Braemar

DERRY LODGE

When Queen Victoria opened the bridge over the Linn of Dee on 8th September 1857, she drank a glass of whisky to its future 'prosperity'. She could never have imagined what that prosperity would mean more than a century later – sightseers crowding the banks of the Linn to see the spectacular waterfalls, cars jamming the approaches to the bridge, and backpacking walkers tramping off into the hills.

The Linn is the gateway to two great Cairngorm passes, the Lairig Ghru and the Lairig an Laoigh. This walk takes you to the doorstep of them both and gives a taste of the mountain massif that sprawls so magnificently between Deeside and Strathspey.

Before setting out, however, it is worth taking a look at the Linn. Here, the River Dee rushes through a narrow channel, only a metre or so wide, cut in the schistose rocks and opening out into a series of great circular pools. Leave your car at the large car park built inside the trees a short distance from the bridge. This is the starting point for the walk.

In the car park are signs saying 'To Derry Lodge'. They mark the start of a shortcut to Glen Lui and the Lodge. Where the shortcut ends, turn left on the track. Now you are in Glen Lui, on the road to Derry, following the Lui Water to the Black Bridge. The first part of the walk is probably the loveliest, with the Lui surging and cascading through a series of beautiful pools, over great rock steps and down turbulent falls. It is in sharp contrast to the bare mountain scenery at the other end of the glen.

The going can be heavy in places, for all along the glen sand and gravel have been laid, which makes for awkward walking. This is supposed to discourage mountain bikes, but they still come, pushing up towards Derry Lodge.

Some people wonder what dark story lies behind the name Black Bridge, but it is called that simply because it was once tarred. Here, as the glen opens up, you go left at the bridge, along a track that was until fairly

INFORMATION

Distance return:
13 km (8 miles).

Start and finish: Linn of Dee, 10 km (6 miles) west of Braemar. There is a large car park near the bridge.

Terrain: Good track all the way, but strong footwear is recommended. Take food and waterproofs.

Refreshments: None en route. Wide selection in Braemar.

Black Bridge in Glen Lui.

recently fringed on one side with ancient pines which spread up the hill slopes on your right. Now they are gone. Watch out for a burn coming down from the right and running under an old stone bridge to join the Lui. You will see a narrow path climbing up the hill. This leads through Clais Fhearnaig to Glen Quoich (see walk 24).

Glen Lui was one of the main routes linking the high passes of the Lairig Ghru and Lairig an Laoigh with Deeside, and as you go up the glen, you pass the ruins of old dwelling-houses at the roadside. The only permanent residents now are the deer. In Glen Lui, if you are lucky, you will see great herds of red deer grazing on the grassy haughs beside the Lui Water. Up on Meall an Lundain, on your right, a line of stags can sometimes be seen on a high ridge anove the track, watching the passing walkers. They will wait until the coast is clear and then come down to join the herd by the river.

Luibeg and the track to the Lairig Ghru.

As you near Derry Lodge, go down a track on the left, across the Lui, where deer often graze outside Luibeg. This remote cottage, now shut up, was once the home of a legendary keeper, Bob Scott, who gave shelter to hundreds of walkers coming out of the Lairig Ghru. They slept in a bothy outside his house, but it was burned down some years ago. A new wooden bothy has been built a little way down the Lui.

Luibeg is a good place to eat your sandwiches and contemplate the Cairngorms. You are on the doorstep of this great mountain range. Across the water, a track winds its way round Carn a'Mhaim on its way into the Lairig Ghru. To the right lies Glen Derry and the Lairig an Laoigh.

It has been said that Lairig Ghru means 'the gloomy pass' and certainly this steep-sided pass, rising to a height of over 800m, can be dark enough. However, the name may come from the Allt Dhru or Druie, the burn on the northern side of the pass which leads down to the great forest of Rothiemurchus and eventually to Aviemore. The Lairig an Laoigh is the pass of cattle, indicating that this was once an important droving route.

Go back to the main track and turn left to Derry Lodge. Not so long ago the approach to it was through a large area of pines, but most of the trees have gone. Derry Lodge itself is boarded up, and the interior is falling into ruin. The lodge was at one time a focal point for hill people. It was leased to the Cairngorm Club for a time in the 1950s, but high rents forced them to give it up.

In the open ground beyond the lodge is a wooden building used by the Aberdeen Mountain Rescue Team, with an emergency telephone on its wall. Nearby, a wooden bridge that spans the Derry Burn has a concrete block with the names of the 19 volunteers who built it. A signpost here points the way to the two Lairigs and back to Braemar.

Leaving the lodge, go back through Glen Lui to the Black Bridge, but instead of crossing it, continue on the track that climbs uphill through the Doire Bhraghad, a fir wood whose name means 'copse of the upland place'. From this hill there is an impressive view looking south up Glen Clunie, while ahead you can see across the Dee to Inverey and the hills beyond it. The lodge at the entrance to Glen Ey and the track pushing south through the glen to Altanour (walk 22) can be picked out as you walk along this 'upland place'.

Above Mar Lodge on the return by Glen Lui.

There is a steep climb after passing the Black Bridge, but it then becomes an easy, pleasant walk. Below, through the trees on the right, is the road from the Linn of Dee to the Linn of Quoich. About 2 km from the Black Bridge a track cuts back and goes downhill, onto the Quoich road. Go right, and a walk of about 1.5 km will take you back to the car park at Linn of Dee.

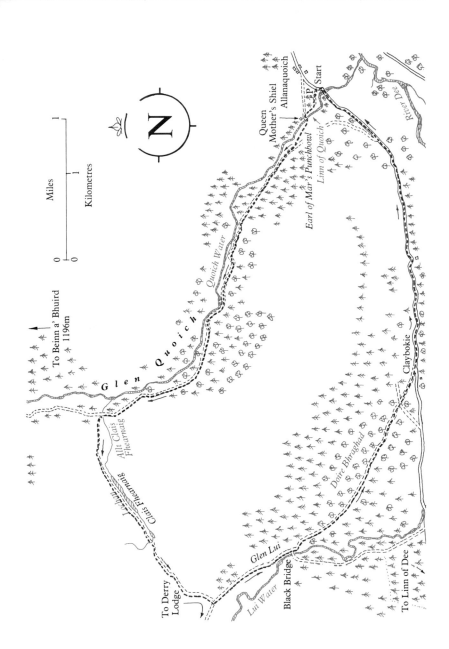

GLEN QUOICH

Although the Linn of Dee is one of Deeside's most popular attractions, another waterfall only 6 km away has its own special appeal. This is the Linn of Quoich, on a tributary of the River Dee, and it is from there that this walk goes to a hidden glen on the edge of the Cairngorms.

The Earl of Mar's Punch Bowl is the starting point. This is a circular hole in one of the rocks that lie in shelves across the Quoich Water. There is a tradition that in 1715 the Earl's men met at the Linn, poured 'ankers of potent Aquavitae' into the Punch Bowl, and drank toasts to the Jacobite cause. The 'bowl' must have had a bottom to it then, for nothing potent comes out of it now. Water, not whisky, pours through the hole as the burn rushes towards the Dee. Apart from its missing bottom, the 'bowl' is perfectly formed, and its shape is best seen when the burn is low.

From the parking area at Allanaquoich, the Linn is only a short distance up the burn, past a red-roofed cottage that is now boarded up. A signpost cautions you to take care on the slippery grass slopes, and in the trees on the right is a ruined cottage which was once a shiel used by the Queen Mother.

A wooden bridge spans the Quoich near the Punch Bowl. It was built in recent years by Scotrail volunteers, replacing a bridge which was on the point of collapse. It provides access to the Punch Bowl from the right (west) bank of the burn and also takes you to a path which links up with the main track going up the Quoich Water by the route you are taking.

INFORMATION

Distance: 14 km (9 miles).

Start and finish: Linn of Quoich. From Braemar take the Linn of Dee road and continue to Linn of Quoich (15 km in total), where there is parking space near the footbridge.

Terrain: Good tracks in Glen Quoich and Glen Lui, but a rough, narrow footpath in Clais Fhearnaig. Boots recommended. Take waterproofs, food and drink.

Refreshments: None en route. Nearest in Braemar.

The Punchbowl at Glen Quoich.

The Linn, shaded by larch and birch trees, is an idyllic spot. The water flows over a blue-green schist which gives it a lovely translucent colour. Its 'big brother' on the Dee may be more spectacular, but the Linn of Quoich has it for beauty.

Follow the path uphill to the main track, which comes up on your left from the road. Turn right, and you are setting out through what Seton Gordon, the distinguished naturalist and writer, called "one of the most delightful glens of the Cairngorms". He gave its name as Gleann Cuaich, the glen of the wooden cup. Some people link this with the rocky quaich or bowl at the Linn, but not all the experts agree.

When you are well up the glen, the great mass of Beinn a'Bhuird comes into view, with the thin finger of a track climbing up over its shoulder. Your route, however, is not to the high tops, but into Clais Fhearnaig, the hidden glen, a pass or ravine lying between Glen Quoich and Glen Lui.

The turning-off point is where the forestry plantation on the left comes to an end, about 5 km from the Linn of Quoich. Look for a burn that is carried under the track by two large pipes. This is the Allt Clais Fhearnaig, the burn that will lead you through the pass to Glen Lui.

Clais Fhearnaig, linking Glen Quoich and Glen Lui.

On the moor, not far from the track, is a small fenced-in field with a rough shed in one corner. On the gate a notice asks walkers to stick to the path during the shooting season. The path, however, is not easy to find, but it can be picked up by following the fence, going left from the gate (the ground here is often wet and muddy) and sticking to it as it turns uphill.

As you near the top of the fence, the path goes off at a '10 o'clock' angle towards a grassy area on the side of the hill, becoming fainter. Cross the grassy area, keeping parallel to the forestry plantation on the left, and you will soon see the path reappearing in front of you.

It drops down into a hollow where a small loch can be seen. The name Clais Fhearnaig actually means 'the hollow of the place of alders', although another interpretation is 'the little glen'. This ravine or cut in the hills is part of a great geological fault running across Scotland. At one time a series of small, rushy pools lay in the hollow. When trout were seen in them many years ago, it was decided to dam the water and make an artificial loch for trout fishing. Trout can still be seen louping from the loch today.

Down by the loch you are cut off from the outside world. Ahead, it looks as if there is no way out. Stunted tree trunks form intricate patterns on the surface and rushes poke slender green fingers up through the water. The 'little glen' is a tranquil place, with only the occasional walker disturbing the peace.

The path pushes along the loch's edge towards what appears to be a dead-end, but as it begins to climb gently uphill another tiny, rush-strewn lochan appears. Beyond it, the moorland opens up and the path, clinging to the hill on the right, heads down into Glen Lui. As you descend you will see the old larachs that are scattered along the glen, a reminder of the days before depopulation. With luck, you will also see the great herds of deer that graze beside the Lui Water.

The path crosses a small burn and finally fades out on the hillside, but it is an easy descent to the Derry Lodge track. When you reach the track, turn left along Glen Lui to the Black Bridge. Don't cross the bridge, but go past it and turn up the track going through the woods of Doire Bhraghad (as in walk 23).

Stick strictly to this track, ignoring any paths going off to the left or right, and it will eventually, in about 3 km, take you down to the road at Claybokie. Turn left and you have an easy 4 km to walk back to the car park at Linn of Quoich.

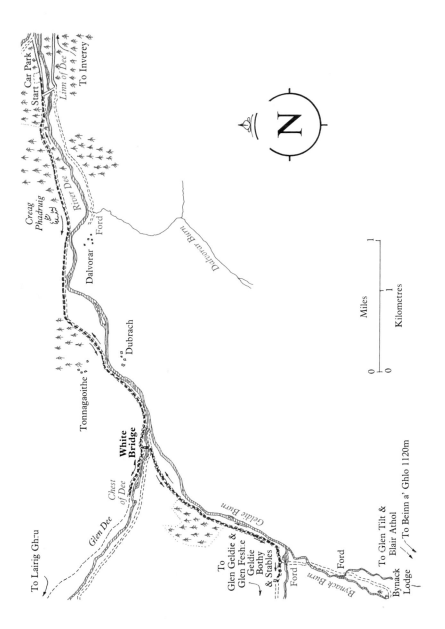

WHITE BRIDGE

Two great passes come together at the White Bridge in Glen Dee. One is the Lairig Ghru leading north to Strathspey, and the other is the pass through Glen Tilt to Blair Atholl. This walk takes you to the junction of the two passes, and gives you a peep into both.

From the Linn of Dee car park, walk back along the road to the Linn and continue straight ahead on the track. There are signs pointing the way to Glen Geldie and Glen Tilt, and a warning that when there are spates, some fords may be impassable.

The track going west to the White Bridge is fringed by pine trees, but those on the left quickly give way to open moorland. The trees on the right hug the track for about 1.5 km, rising up the slopes below Craig Phadruig. Eagles have been known to nest in this pine belt, within a kilometre of the picnic parties and tourist coaches at the Linn.

On the opposite bank of the Dee another track can be seen, but it runs out at a ford across the Dee where the Dalvorar Burn comes down from the hills. There are ruins of old settlements on both sides of the river, and those at Dalvorar have a small place in the history books. Dalvorar is from the Gaelic Dail a'Mhorair, the haugh of the nobleman, but what nobleman give his name to it nobody knows. Perhaps it was Viscount Dundee, who is said to have camped here with his troops 14 days before the Battle of Killiecrankie in 1689.

Here, too, the swollen Dee raged across the glen in the floods of 1829, known as the Muckle Spate. The waters swept around the farmhouse at Dalvorar so quickly that the farmer, his wife and seven children barely had time to make their escape. They waded away from their home and tramped through the storm to Inverey. Today, the spates still come, as the warning notice at the Linn of Dee reminds us, but they are seldom as angry as the Muckle Spate of 1829.

One ruin on the right of the track has the name of Tonnagaoithe. It is supposed to come from the Gaelic

INFORMATION

Distance return: 16 km (10 miles).

Start and finish: Linn of Dee car park, 10 km west of Braemar.

Terrain: Good track to White Bridge, though in places it has been covered in sand and gravel, making for slightly uncomfortable walking. Boots or strong shoes recommended. Take waterproofs, food and drink.

Refreshments: None en route. Nearest in Braemar.

Stag at the roadside on way to Linn of Dee.

Ton na Gaoithe, meaning 'bottom of the wind', but Dr Adam Watson and Elizabeth Allan, in their book *The Place Names of Upper Deeside*, give a ruder translation. They say it was 'translated to us as "winy airse", which is Scots for "windy arse"'.

Bridge at Linn of Dee.

On the south side of the river, 3 km from the Linn of Dee, are the remains of Dubrach, which also has historical associations. 'Dubrach' was the by-name of Peter Grant, the oldest rebel in the 1745 Jacobite Rising, whose father was a tenant of the farm in Glen Dee. Peter lived to be 110 years old and, ironically, was given a pension by King George IV. They say that when 'Dubrach' was buried in Braemar kirkyard, four gallons of whisky were drunk 'even before the lifting'.

The farm of Dubrach was also the setting for one of Upper Deeside's most baffling mysteries. After the 1745 Rising, a guard of Hanoverian soldiers under the command of Sergeant Arthur Davies was quartered at the farm. In September 1749, while on his way to Altanour in Glen Ey, Sgt Davies disappeared. The following year his body was found in the Glen Ey area.

The White Bridge spans the Dee about a kilometre past Dubrach. The track across it goes south by the Geldie Burn, but before you cross the bridge, look for a signpost indicating a public footpath which goes up Glen Dee to the Lairig Ghru and on to Rothiemurchus and Aviemore. About 700m along this track is the Chest of Dee, where the river flows over a series of rock shelves above clear, deep pools. The Chest, or Kist, which is well worth a detour, can also be reached by a bulldozed track on the opposite side of the river. The picturesque pools can be seen from either side, but the Lairig Ghru path is the best place from which to take photographs.

From the Chest of Dee you look up to the Devil's Point and the mouth of the Lairig Ghru, while back at the White Bridge the Geldie draws you down towards Bynack and Glen Tilt. So here the two great passes lie on each side of you – the Lairig Ghru, which the writer H. V. Morton described as 'an early Italian painter's idea of hell', and Glen Tilt, which Thomas Pennant said was 'the most dangerous and most horrible I have ever travelled'.

There is nothing white today about the White Bridge, although it was said to be painted that colour at one time, but oddly enough the Gaelic name for the Geldie is geal dhe, the White Dee. Cross the bridge and follow the track as it runs between the Geldie Burn and a plantation of trees on your right.

This was a well-beaten drovers' path and if events had taken a different turn it might have become a motor road from Strathspey to Deeside. In the 18th century, General George Wade contemplated a road link from Ruthven Barracks, near Kingussie, through Glen Feshie and Glen Geldie to Braemar, and his 20th century successors also had a dream in their minds of a fast tourist highway from west to east. Happily, nothing came of it.

The Geldie comes bouncing in from the west. There is a signpost pointing to Glen Geldie and also south to Blair Atholl by Glen Tilt. The track turns right to Glen Geldie and Glen Feshie, passing a ruined red-roofed building, all that is left of the Lower Geldie cottage and stables. Across from the cottage, broken pillars mark the site of the former bridge over the Geldie. Now, walkers going south through Glen Tilt (or coming the other way) have to cross by fording the river, which in winter can be ravaged by the spates that brought the bridge down.

From the ford a cluster of trees can be seen across the river about 1.5 km away. They shelter the ruins of Bynack Lodge, where Queen Victoria stopped for tea on her way back to Balmoral from Blair Atholl. The Lodge was said at one time to be haunted by a poltergeist.

From the Geldie stables you can look down Glen Tilt and see mighty Beinn a'Ghlo rising up in the distance. It will be your last view before you turn and head back to the White Bridge and the track to Linn of Dee.

Bynack stables at Glen Geldie.

INDEX

HMSO publications are available from:

HMSO Bookshops
71 Lothian Road, Edinburgh, EH3 9AZ
031-228 4181 Fax 031-229 2734
49 High Holborn, London, WC1V 6HB
071-873 0011 Fax 071-873 8200 (counter service only)
258 Broad Street, Birmingham, B1 2HE
021-643 3740 Fax 021-643 6510
33 Wine Street, Bristol, BS1 2BQ
0272 264306 Fax 0272 294515
9-21 Princess Street, Manchester, M60 8AS
061-834 7201 Fax 061-833 0634
16 Arthur Street, Belfast, BT1 4GD
0232 238451 Fax 0232 235401

HMSO Publications Centre
(Mail, fax and telephone orders only)
PO Box 276, London, SW8 5DT
Telephone orders 071-873 9090
General enquiries 071-873 0011
(queuing system in operation for both numbers)
Fax orders 071-873 8200

HMSO's Accredited Agents
(see Yellow Pages)

and through good booksellers

Other titles in this series

25 Walks – Highland Perthshire
25 Walks – The Trossachs

Other titles in preparation

25 Walks – Fife
25 Walks – Galloway
25 Walks – The Border Hills
25 Walks – In and Around Edinburgh
25 Walks – In and Around Glasgow

Long distance guides published by HMSO

The West Highland Way – Official Guide
The Southern Upland Way – Official Guide

Printed in Scotland for HMSO by CC No. 45489 50C 4/94